The Craft of Strategy Formation

The Craft of Strategy Formation

Translating business issues into
actionable strategies

Eric Wiebes, Marc Baaij, Bas Keibek
and Pieter Witteveen

John Wiley & Sons, Ltd

Other Wiley Editorial Offices

John Wiley & Sons Inc., 111 River Street, Hoboken, NJ 07030, USA

Jossey-Bass, 989 Market Street, San Francisco, CA 94103-1741, USA

Wiley-VCH Verlag GmbH, Boschstr. 12, D-69469 Weinheim, Germany

John Wiley & Sons Australia Ltd, 42 McDougall Street, Milton, Queensland 4064, Australia

John Wiley & Sons (Asia) Pte Ltd, 2 Clementi Loop #02-01, Jin Xing Distripark, Singapore 129809

John Wiley & Sons Canada Ltd, 6045 Freemont Blvd, Mississauga, ONT, L5R 4J3, Canada

Wiley also publishes its books in a variety of electronic formats. Some content that appears in print may not be available in electronic books.

Anniversary Logo Design: Richard J. Pacifico

British Library Cataloguing in Publication Data

A catalogue record for this book is available from the British Library

ISBN 978-0-470-51859-5 (HB)

Translated from Dutch by Michelle Wilbraham

Typeset in 11/16pt Trump Medieval by SNP Best-set Typesetter Ltd., Hong Kong
Printed and bound in Great Britain by TJ International Ltd, Padstow, Cornwall, UK
This book is printed on acid-free paper responsibly manufactured from sustainable forestry in which at least two trees are planted for each one used for paper production.

Contents

Preface   **vii**

Introduction   **xi**
  What is this book all about?   xi
  Introduction to the Allware case study   xxv

Part I – The preparation phase   **1**
Introduction   3

  1 Days 1 to 5 – We create a question out of
     a concern   7
  2 Days 6 and 7 – We set up a project organisation   27
  3 Day 8 – We structure the question   39
  4 Day 9 – We formulate hypotheses   51
  5 Day 10 – We make a work plan   57
  6 Allware: the first two weeks   79

Part II – The analysis phase   **89**
Introduction   91

 7   Days 11 and 12 – We develop the analyses further   95
 8   Days 13 to 17 – We collect data   117
 9   Days 18 to 42 – We carry out the analyses   135
10   Days 43 to 45 – We present the conclusions   149
11   Allware: on with the analysis   171

Part III – The decision-making phase   **181**
Introduction   183

12   Day 46 – We put forward a few business options   185
13   Day 47 – We set up scenarios   193
14   Days 48 to 57 – We model the results   199
15   Days 58 to 60 – We choose the strategic direction   209
16   Days 61 to 65 – We write the strategic plan   215
17   Allware: make a choice and carry on   221

Part IV – The implementation phase   **225**
Introduction   227

18   Set up an organisation to implement the strategy   231
19   Draw up the implementation plan   237
20   Direct progress   247

Afterword   **259**

Profile of OC&C Strategy Consultants   **263**

Index   **267**

Preface

Insight into a modern craft

Few people have had the privilege, like the authors of this book, to have worked for decades as professional strategy consultants. The question is still asked, with some justification, whether strategy consultancy really is a profession. After all, anyone can call themselves a consultant and what do these men and women actually do? In our case (the firm OC&C Strategy Consultants) we take this profession very seriously. Teams from our firm always work in close cooperation with our clients to strengthen the position of their company or institute and to create value for shareholders, other interested parties or for society as a whole. It is inspiring work; work that gives you a lot back when you put in a lot of effort. Contact with clients, contact with young members of staff and the kick that you get from providing new solutions – all these factors together make the work an inspiration.

When Marc Baaij, Associate Professor of Strategic Management at RSM Erasmus University in Rotterdam, approached OC&C to ask whether we might like to write a book with him about our profession and how we go about our work, we had to ponder the matter for a while. Is it a sensible idea to distil all our knowledge in a book? Our profession is losing its mystique and wouldn't we just be opening the door to competitors, allowing them to take over aspects of our philosophy and acquire some of our practical skills? Can we describe our experience in such a way that the confidentiality of our relations with clients remains our top priority?

As the book before you shows, we gave a positive answer to the question. We are convinced that strategy consultancy is not only a fantastic profession, but also a craft that you can only put into practice if your firm has excellent systems, training and – most importantly – carefully selected and carefully developed staff. It is less easy to copy than it might seem. What is more, if this book leads to more of our fellow firms doing better work, then we don't mind at all. The profession does not always have an equally positive reputation and if this book can help to improve that reputation – great! More important, however, than the reasons given above is that we want to make strategy formulation comprehensible to our clients. It is often not necessary to work intensively with a consultant. We find it enjoyable, inspiring and we believe that the company's results improve significantly, but in many cases in-house teams can do the job. This book is aimed precisely at those in-house teams. We offer them a helping hand in dealing, in a creative but well-structured way, with questions that determine the future of their company or institution.

It was a privilege for us to work on this book. Marc Baaij the scientist was snowed under with material from enthusiastic consultants who had put down on paper their everyday experience, their intellectual breakthroughs and the lessons they had learnt. We hope that the book is suitable for a broad-based target group, thanks to its combination of theoretical insights and our practical approach. Top of the list, as we have already said, are those who are actively involved in forming strategies: leaders of large and medium-sized companies and institutions. At the same time the book offers a practical insight to those who are engaged in a management study. Many theoretical frameworks that deal with strategy have been developed but up to now there has been no description of how you can actually, concretely, put a strategy into practice. Henry Mintzberg has tried to describe what managers do in practice. Thus we have attempted to explain what strategy makers do.

A final word of thanks goes to all our colleagues in our global network, who worked selflessly on this book. They contributed examples, listed dos and don'ts, read, reread and edited manuscripts. It became a real company exercise. The creation of this book was in itself a strategic undertaking: before we started we had a few structures in mind and putting these into practice led us onto other paths. We hope that readers will enjoy similar experiences and that their work will be the more interesting for it!

Eric Wiebes, Marc Baaij, Bas Keibek and
Pieter Witteveen

Introduction

What is this book all about?

This book is about strategy, but after reading it you still won't know where to take your organisation. The word strategy appears on average on every page, but you won't come across a single usable strategic recommendation. We do not know whether your organisation should focus on its core competences, whether vertical integration will create value, or whether global brands are the future. We cannot know that because we do not know your organisation – and who believes in generic recipes anyway? This book is a step-by-step manual on how you the reader can best develop a strategy.

Formulating a strategy isn't just a matter of holding a brainstorming session. You may have to wrestle with a flood of figures or, conversely, find that your strategy formulation suffers from a lack of data. We see analyses that offer no insights and we encounter conclusions that are not based on facts. We meet strategies that are not at all, or not sufficiently, different from those of the competition, or that are simply not achievable. These problems are linked to the method used to formulate the strategy. This book is not about the correct strategy for an organisation. It is about the correct *method* for formulating a strategy. We do not use any standard frameworks – we describe step by step the whole strategy-formulation process. This is the method that we have been using for years on behalf of our clients, prominent organisations from around the world. Although every consultancy firm will claim to have its own unique method, the approaches of a limited number of top strategy companies are broadly similar. This is the cookbook of the top chefs in strategyland: the top strategy consultants.

We all know more or less what is meant by strategy. There is no need to repeat here a dozen different definitions of strategy from the scientific literature. We do not need any examples from the Mesopotamians, the ancient Chinese or Greeks, or quotes from Machiavelli or Von Clausewitz. Strategy is what the organisation wants to achieve and how.

It would, however, be a good idea to elaborate a little on the concept of strategy. The authors of this book hold a number of outspoken views on strategy and strategy development. These views form the basis of the method laid out in this book. Anyone who does not share these views will not gain as much from this book and may even find themselves occasionally getting annoyed about the content. For this reason we shall clarify our views below.

A specific explanation of strategy . . .

In this book we focus mainly on competitive or *business unit* strategy. Questions of *corporate* strategy are not explicitly addressed here, although the method can certainly be applied in general terms to such corporate matters. We shall summarise our views on business unit strategy by listing them in order of importance. Anyone who feels their skin crawl as soon as they start this list had better put the book down. If you still feel fine when you reach the end of the list, it's safe to go ahead. The following concepts form the basis of this book:

Corporate strategy versus *business unit* strategy

By business unit strategy we mean the way in which an organisation competes in a specific business sector. This strategy embraces all the choices made regarding products or services, clients, prices, distribution channels, production methods and everything else necessary to gain a strong competitive position in a market or in a number of interconnected markets. The business unit strategy demands pure strategic thinking, in which theory is at its most advanced and the business unit manager can make use of clear, undeniable logic. Think, for example, of the various concepts and frameworks of Porter, Prahalad and others.

Corporate strategy (or group strategy) concerns the course taken by the diversified organisation as a whole, which transcends the business unit level. It includes the optimal size and composition of the business portfolio and the role of the holding company in relation to the coordination and integration of the business units that constitute it. This subject area has been much discussed and exhaustively studied, but it has been less well worked out and it is subject to more controversy, not least due to its greater complexity.

- *Strategy is focused on the creation of value for the organisation*

  Someone who does not have a clear goal does not need a strategy either. A strategy aims to achieve, well, something. What it achieves is determined by the organisation itself. It can be value for shareholders, greater safety on the streets, or good quality drinking water for minimal costs per unit. Less concrete aims such as 'the continuity of the organisation' or 'a better existence for all stakeholders' just don't make the grade. Beware also of the extremely popular 'What kind of organisation do we want to be in the future?' What kind of organisation we want to be cannot, after all, be used as a starting point. It is at most an outcome of the question as to how we can create value in the future.

- *A strategy is more than a vision or a mission*

  A vision can form the basis of a chosen strategy, but a vision does not always tell us *what* should be done. A vision also often lacks a firm foundation – how do we know that the vision will really lead to better results? A mission can be a persuasive way of putting across the main points of a strategy, but it does not state how we want to achieve our goal. A strategy tells us two things: *what* we want to achieve and *how*.

- *A strategy is focused on winning the competition game*

  Whether yours is a commercial or a not-for-profit organisation, it makes no sense for you to aim to do things (almost) as well as the others. A commercial organisation that underperforms a competitor invites investors to put their money elsewhere. Non-profit organisations that perform less well than their fellows demonstrate that their idealistic goals are better left to others to achieve, or that other organisations realise their aims more efficiently. A strategy indicates how we think that we can win the game. There are two ways to win the game against the competitors in your field. The first is to play the same game better. Porter calls this 'operational effectiveness'. The second is to play a different game from your competitors. 'Better' or 'different' are both acceptable options, but it is not our ambition just to do as well as the others.

- *A strategy demands choices*

  Someone who does not need to choose, does not need a strategy. They just go ahead and do. It is difficult to develop a strategy because it requires choices, often amid uncertainty and unknown factors, and these choices commit the organisation to long-term, substantial investments. A choice now has consequences for the future. Strategy is based on commitment, because these choices cannot simply be undone. Strategy also means deciding what *not* to do. We *will* do this but we *won't* do that.

- *A strategy is all-encompassing*

  Everything is called strategy. Admittedly, we also sometimes talk of the 'commercial strategy' or the 'distribution
  strategy', but these are names for non-existent concepts.
  It suggests that there is such a thing as a separate distribution strategy. However, the way in which we organise
  distribution is connected to how we run the rest of the
  organisation. Characteristics of our distribution (for
  example, good access to small clients) may be reasons for
  developing particular products (for example, smaller office
  machines). On the other hand, the presence of these products may prompt the expansion of distribution to small
  clients (for example, through intermediaries). A 'product
  strategy' without tackling distribution is unthinkable, but
  an approach to distribution without matching products is
  also meaningless. From now on, when we mention distribution strategy we mean the approach to distribution
  within the strategy. The strategy applies to all business
  methods, aspects and tools. It is precisely a characteristic
  of strategy that it transcends all functional disciplines
  and integrates them. The strategy is therefore primarily
  the responsibility of senior management not, in the first
  instance, of functional management.

... and an outspoken view on how strategy should be developed ...

Not all cookbooks are the same. The foundation of this 'cookbook' for developing a strategy is a set of three choices. Other
choices would also have been possible, as a strategy may be

developed in all sorts of ways, but we have achieved the best results with this method.

We choose the hypothesis-driven 'problem-solving' approach

Although there is a natural tendency to investigate 'everything', we favour a problem-focused approach. Our method does not automatically begin with a thorough analysis of the organisation's external environment (the business sector and the macro environment) in its entirety, or its internal management in all its elements. Our method doesn't prescribe any standard analytical concepts or frameworks; we apply them as soon as they appear to be needed.

The steps to be followed in our method are determined by the problem at hand. We let ourselves be led by the challenge faced by the organisation. This can be an acute crisis in which the destruction of value must be reversed, but it can also be a situation in which the organisation is performing extremely well but wants to develop new sources of value with an eye to a future, such as market saturation, technological advances or deregulation.

A *problem-solving* approach moves from the broad picture to the particular. As advisors we always focus on the most important and most likely causes of the problem or opportunities for improvement. These hypotheses receive all our attention. Other possible causes and opportunities are not considered, at least not initially. This makes the thinking process efficient, but of course we cannot completely exclude the possibility that these hypotheses may turn out to be incorrect. However, these hypotheses can always be rejected when tested, in other words when analysed. We therefore use an iterative process in which new hypotheses can be introduced. In addition, the outcome of certain analyses can make another, planned analysis superfluous. The hypothesis-driven *problem-solving* approach thus requires a flexible plan of work.

A chain of fashion stores can serve as an example here. In order to determine where the greatest potential for improving results lies, we consider, for example, the margin, and the turnover and costs per square metre of shop floor space. If we then find that costs are in line with those of a number of well-performing competitors, and that these costs have not increased excessively, we can assume that the best chances for improvement will not be found in the area of costs. That is of course not certain. It could be that our rental costs are relatively low, but staff costs are unnecessarily high, so that there are also possibilities for change in the area of costs. Perhaps we should then break down the costs, for example into staff, rental and energy costs. However, even then the answer is not certain. The *problem-solving* approach sets out from the premise that we cannot investigate everything, but that we must make choices as to what we focus on. The conclusions of a problem-solving approach are very probable, but they are not certain. It is a matter of having a sufficient level of probability. The *problem-solving* approach recognises that we do not have to and indeed cannot investigate 'everything', but that we must make choices as to what we focus our attention on.

We use facts as a basis for conclusions, quantified wherever possible

'You can prove anything with figures' is a saying that aims to mean the opposite of what it says. We would rather say: without figures it is very difficult to prove anything. We are naturally aware of the fact that not everything can be expressed in numbers, but we strive to substantiate our conclusions as much as possible in quantifiable terms. The facts and figures tell the true story, which sometimes contradicts the picture that emerges from interviews or from a 'gut feeling'. A look at the figures to see what is going on can often lead to surprising or shocking discoveries. The facts often turn out to be more fascinating than all the stories going around. We also lay great store by numbers, not because figures tell the whole story, but because an argument without any figures so often gives an incorrect or too vague a picture. Someone who cannot differentiate between great and small is also in danger of losing sight of the difference between important and unimportant matters.

The team works in a pressure cooker

In this book, the strategy development process is described along a timeline of the length of a typical strategy consulting project: three months (or 65 working days). To develop a strategy in three months is actually a mad idea. However, it is often even crazier to remove key workers from their positions for longer than three months. From a purely rational point of view it may sometimes be justifiable to spend a year thinking about a strategy with officials recruited specially for that purpose, but so rarely does anything come of it, it delivers so little in the way of results.

We have seen very good results from our approach under great time pressure. Time pressure imposes discipline; it forces people to make choices and focuses the attention on essentials. It prevents overly theoretical detours that divert attention from the most critical questions. A strategy cannot of course be implemented in three months, but we do not make that claim.

Why three months?

Developing a strategy in three months. It sounds a lot like losing 10 kilos in three weeks. How do you know that three months is the appropriate period for *any* strategy, for *every* strategy? Wouldn't it be possible to go much faster in one case, or might it not take more time in another case? Why three months?

Speed is an *asset*. Not only because working fast means that one is ready sooner, but also because speed has an intrinsic value in the *problem-solving* process. Speed imposes discipline, it forces one to choose the really relevant analyses. Speed ensures that from the outset the team members make an estimate as to the outcome, which sometimes means discovering that further analysis is pointless. Speed creates enthusiasm and momentum, it brings team members closer together and makes us awake and alert. The leading strategic advice firms move quickly, and not only to limit costs. In a strategic project we must aim for that healthy acceleration of the heartbeat that accompanies a tight deadline.

Without a deadline there is no momentum. You can carry out a comparative cost analysis in three days, if you keep your options open and are endowed with a good feel for real relationships. But you can just as easily take a week to do it and we would not seek to contradict anyone who claims that a month is needed. But anyone who really wants to do a good job – and after all, who doesn't want to do a good job – will take a year. Without a deadline three days become a week, or a month, or a year.

To return to the question: is three months the appropriate length of time? The answer is usually no, but you only know that *after* the event. In many cases three months is a very good estimate to make *before* you begin. And you have to set a deadline at the start, otherwise it isn't a deadline. We have completed many, sometimes complex, strategy projects in three months. Not that there weren't any details left to be filled in. Not that there weren't any questions left outstanding. However, at the end of three months there *was* something in place, the direction was clear, surprises had been uncovered and new truths for-mulated. Most business units shouldn't need more than three months to develop a new but not overly exotic strategy.

In any case this book is based on the three-month period. It gives an idea of the length of time needed for the various steps. It may be that from the start the three-month format is not compatible with the natural heartbeat of the organisation, or that the project is clearly far too complex. You can then adjust the time period. Before you start. Because then it is a deadline and we naturally want to respect the deadline. Be flexible with the initial planning and stick firmly to it afterwards.

. . . deliver an approach that is more than just 'a bit of logical thinking'

The concept of strategy described above and the approach that we described are – whether or not you agree with them – not overly complex. We have employed this approach in our firm for many years and we have never been secretive about it with our clients. There is no question of an industrial secret or a patented method. Every element of the approach is logical and defensible, and the consequences for the process can be worked out with a little thought. Thus, you could almost say that with 'a bit of logical thinking' (the popular stereotype for strategic advice), everyone must be able to follow this method.

How is this book constructed?

This book offers a step-by-step explanation of the strategy-development process. This comprises four phases (see Figure 0.1), of which in fact only the first three fit into the aforementioned three months. After these three months (65 working days) there is a well-founded strategic plan in place. Each phase is divided into a number of

	Preparation	Analysis	Decision-making	Implementation
Activities	• Define scope & central question • Appoint project team • Structure problem • Form hypotheses • Draw up work plan	• Design analyses • Collect data • Carry out analyses and test results • Draw conclusions • Pull together results & present findings	• Draw up business options • Define scenarios • Model financial implications • Discuss projections • Include choices in business plan	• Work out practical implications • Draw up implementation plan • Appoint implementation team • Implementation & monitoring
End products	• Concrete strategic question • Project team • Work plan and hypotheses	• Answers to key questions of work plan • 'Evidence' • Recommendations for specific elements of the strategic challenge	• Business plan • Financial projections	• Implementation plan • Implementation team • → Strategy implemented

Figure 0.1 Formulating strategy in four phases – the structure of the book

concrete, feasible steps. In the preparation phase (two weeks) we convert a concern into a question, then structure the question, elaborate hypotheses, set up a project organisation, and outline a plan of action. In the analysis phase (seven weeks) we develop the analyses further, gather the data, carry out the analyses and present the conclusions. In the selection phase (four weeks) we draw up a number of business options, we define a number of scenarios, choose a strategic direction and make a business plan. In the implementation phase we set up the implementation organisation, draw up an implementation plan and supervise progress.

We also give an example using a specific company. The book describes the development of a strategy for the technical wholesaler, Allware, first introducing the company then reporting after each phase on the results achieved at Allware as a result of our approach.

We have noticed, however, that after we have gone it is not always easy for organisations to apply our approach to other strategic questions (we hope that they have less trouble with the strategy developed for them). It is hard to develop focus, to be concrete and to give quantified underpinning to visionary ideas. Even for us as a firm it takes a few years as a rule for junior colleagues to become completely comfortable with our approach. It seems the approach is easy to understand but not so easy to master. The fact-based *problem-solving* method in a pressure cooker should, it appears, be seen as a real craft. And crafts require practice. Even those who have a talent for a craft have to learn it. Few are born with such a skill.

Learning to cook begins with a good cookery book. If you want to learn this approach, you will have to try it out a few times. This book gives a helping hand in that direction. Follow the recipe and 'feel' how it goes. Work in a team, as a team gets stuck less often than an individual. Pay attention to the method and the process as well as the content of the strategy, because the content places demands on the method and the process. Take courage if things don't go quite as expected. This book aims to shorten the learning process but an instant result is unrealistic.

Good luck!

Introduction to the Allware case study

1 September 2006 – a hectic start

Jenny Michaels, 29 years old, is a mechanical engineer but she had also just gained an MBA from a prominent business school. Today is the first day of her post-MBA career. Her new employer Allware had created the post of Vice President Strategy and Business Development especially for her. Full of energy and drive, and with a head full of up-to-date knowledge about *value chains*, *real options* and *product lifecycle management* theories, Jenny has reported this morning to her new boss – Allware CEO Joseph Schmidt – only to be stopped at the door of his office by his secretary. Mr Schmidt is in a crisis meeting with his directors and representatives of the Kuhn family (founders and majority shareholders in Allware). Would Jenny please wait in her new office until he has time for her.

Three hours later Schmidt comes in, looking concerned. 'Welcome Jenny, and sorry to have kept you waiting,' he says, 'but we have a big problem. The new half-year results have been announced today and they look bad. The family demands that we sort things out. If things aren't any better in six months, we might as well clear our desks. I know that you have plans for introducing balanced score cards and improving business planning, but I'm afraid that those will have to wait. You must help me and my colleagues on the board to get this company swiftly back on track. It's lucky you know everything about strategy. We'll really need that.'

Five minutes later Schmidt closes the door behind him, leaving Jenny feeling rather overwhelmed. He has asked her to develop a new strategy for Allware in three months, he has given her carte blanche to tackle the problem however she sees fit and promised her the full cooperation of all Allware companies and departments. It is a wonderful opportunity for Jenny to put her newly acquired MBA know-how into practice and to prove herself in her new position. But where to begin? Three months? And she doesn't even know the company yet!

Allware – products, clients and geographical distribution

Jenny's new employer Allware is an international wholesaler in pumps, gaskets and valves. These are technical products that are used wherever pipes and hoses are to be found, from large chemical factories to the central heating in ordinary homes. The products vary in size from a few centimetres to one metre in diameter, from 200 grams to one tonne in weight, and from a few euros to tens of thousands of euros in value. Products from all over the world, from famous names in manufacturing to small, specialised factories in Germany and Sweden. Allware sells and distributes these products in various countries, to many different sorts of clients (see Figure 0.2).

The half-year results – symptoms of the problem

Schmidt has given Jenny the new half-year results and it is true that they do not look very good. Turnover is stagnating

Allware, breakdown of sales
(€m)

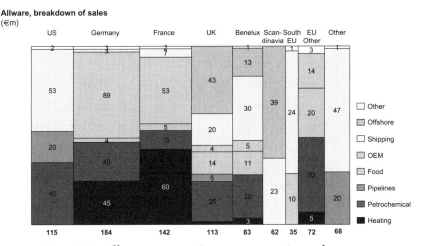

Figure 0.2 Allware operates in many countries and sectors

and profits are under great pressure because sales and operational costs have risen sharply. The problem also appears to be fairly universal. Results have worsened in nearly all countries and market segments. Remarks by the group's financial controller on the figures also give little room for optimism: 'The intended reversal of last year's downward trend has not been achieved. With the exception of the USA, none of the country budgets will be balanced. The measures that the various country managers put into place at the beginning of this year do not appear to be working. Analyses of the underlying figures confirm the gravity of the situation. Clients – particularly major ones – are leaving. The departures of Giant Chemicals and Pantagruel Shipbuilding in particular were heavy blows. A number of important agencies – such as Augeas Pumping – have been lost. Sales costs have risen further in spite of the staff reductions that we have carried out. Only the steady margin, which we have been able to maintain despite the unfavourable economic conditions, gives us any reason for satisfaction.'

Jenny's strategic solution: to be continued

You will be able to read how Jenny Michaels works out a radical new strategy for Allware later in this book. At the end of each phase our approach will be illustrated with the help of Jenny's experiences. Each time we will focus on a number of elements and activities – a complete description would be going too far. We hope that this case study will clarify the approach we use. It will in any case demonstrate that a standard approach is pointless; the process is adapted as soon as the findings make it necessary.

Part I – The preparation phase

Introduction

BUYERS OF SOFTWARE ARE STILL OFTEN ADVISED TO READ the instructions before using their new package. Skiing organisations advise their members to start doing exercises weeks before their trip. And anyone who bakes a cake will read in the cookery book that they should first have all the ingredients ready and sieve the flour. Of course nobody actually does any of this. We simply switch the computer on and see how far we get, give our legs a quick stretch shortly before we hit the slopes, and tip the flour, unsieved, straight into the cake mix. Preparation is boring, and who has time for it?

In a strategy project the preparation phase (see Figure I.1) cannot be missed out, but this phase is not at all boring. It is

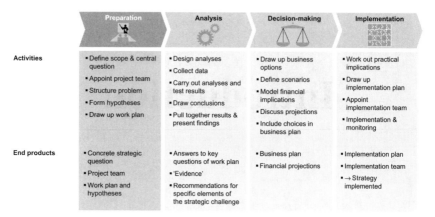

Figure I.1 Phase 1: preparation

not necessary to read this whole handbook; there are no exercises to be done and no ingredients to be got ready. In the preparation phase it is necessary to start thinking deeply from the outset. To a great extent this phase determines the outcome. What is the problem, what are the real questions and what are we going to look at?

Those very people who have little time or enthusiasm for such activities must give the preparation phase their best shot. In this phase we will, among other things, decide what we are not going to look at and what we are not going to do. Anyone who wants to develop a strategy in three months would be well advised to make this list as long as possible. The preparation phase frees up more time than it requires if you do it properly. In strategic terms: a good preparation is a profitable investment (see Figure I.2).

At the end of five working days we expect to have the following end products:

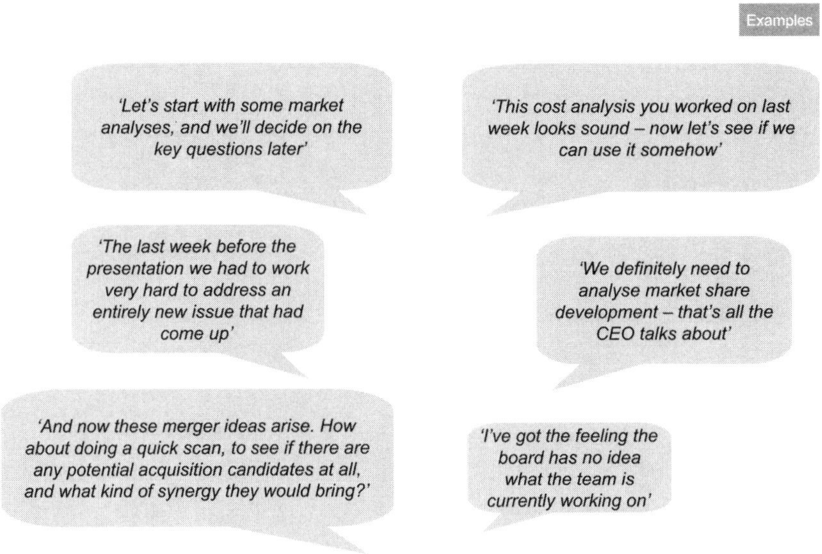

'Let's start with some market analyses, and we'll decide on the key questions later'

'This cost analysis you worked on last week looks sound – now let's see if we can use it somehow'

'The last week before the presentation we had to work very hard to address an entirely new issue that had come up'

'We definitely need to analyse market share development – that's all the CEO talks about'

'And now these merger ideas arise. How about doing a quick scan, to see if there are any potential acquisition candidates at all, and what kind of synergy they would bring?'

'I've got the feeling the board has no idea what the team is currently working on'

Examples

Figure I.2 There are sometimes clear signals that there has been insufficient preparation

- A concrete strategic question, based on what was at first no more than a vague concern

- An overview of the most important hypotheses and subsidiary questions

- A clear work plan, with tasks and deadlines

- A team of motivated individuals, with sufficient time and capabilities to do the job.

1

Days 1 to 5 – We create a question out of a concern

What is our goal for this week?

Many strategic projects start with a feeling that 'something is wrong here'. Profit is disappointing, the market is changing or we want to grow but we don't know how. Then there is the question: 'Where do we want to take the organisation?' A good question but not very concrete. A question like this gives you the feeling of being fobbed off. If the question is not a concrete one, nearly every answer is correct, but no single answer is really usable.

The basis of the problem-solving approach is the well-put central question: 'What do we actually want to solve here?' That is today's goal: to translate a vague concern into a concrete, central question. If the questioner cannot make the question concrete, then whoever is going to answer the question will have to do it.

Why is it really so important to formulate a concrete, central question? Surely we can just look at the business? The answer is no – that doesn't work. Without a question there can never be an answer, work is never finished, there is always more to do and there is always somebody who asks: 'Have you looked at this, then?'

There are of course occasions when a concrete, central question is already present at the start of the project. Even in these cases, though, we do not completely skip the first five days.

The answer is 42

There was a moment's expectant pause while panels slowly came to life on the front of the console. Lights flashed on and off experimentally and settled down into a businesslike pattern. A soft low hum came from the communication channel.

'Good morning,' said Deep Thought at last.

– 'Er . . . good morning, O Deep Thought,' said Loonquawl nervously, 'do you have . . . er, that is, . . .'

'An Answer for you?' interrupted Deep Thought majestically. 'Yes. I have.'

The two men shivered with expectancy. Their waiting had not been in vain.

– 'There really is one? . . . To the great Question of Life, the Universe and Everything? . . . We must know it now! Now!'

. . .

'All right,' said the computer . . . 'The Answer to the Great Question . . . of Life, the Universe and Everything . . . is . . . forty-two . . .'

. . . It was a long time before anyone spoke . . .

– 'Forty-two!' yelled Loonquawl. 'Is that all you've got to show for seven and a half million years' work?'

'I checked it very thoroughly,' said the computer, . . .

Source: Douglas Adams, *The Hitchhiker's Guide to the Galaxy.*

When a concrete question is lacking

At international business schools students learn through bitter experience that an answer only exists if there is a concrete question. On day one the students are put together in groups to ponder a company's situation. With piles of paper under their arms they disappear in groups of six into rooms with the task of giving a presentation the following morning on the future of the company. Heated brainstorming sessions follow. Evening falls. There are discussions. Team members don't agree with one another. As night approaches some groups still have nothing down on paper.

Next morning the lecturer welcomes a class full of sullen students, with bags under their eyes, who give talks that show clear signs of having been written in haste. The conclusions are not always equally clear, the talk is often too long. What went wrong? Among other things: there was no concrete question.

Do we really know for sure that the question provided is the real question? Take the board of a listed company that thinks its falling share price is due to the fact that the financial markets do not sufficiently understand and value the firm's strategy. The concrete question then becomes: 'How can we convince the financial markets of the value of our strategy?' The real problem may lie not in communication with the financial markets, but rather in the strategy itself: the strategy is just no good. Or take a situation where the questioner has a personal interest in having the question posed differently. For political reasons they would like the real question to be left alone. Preparation is just as essential in situations where a question already exists. We must test the existing questions thoroughly before we adopt them. Incorrect questions lead to unusable answers.

In order to track down the central question, we first limit the area to be searched so that we can then look specifically for starting points for the question. During this search we look in particular at differences (between the existing performance and the norm, between ourselves and the competition) and changes (in the market, in competitors' behaviour).

What are the steps to be taken?

Step 1   Leave out everything that is irrelevant

When we start to think about business strategy we often don't know what to focus on, but we are often clear about what we definitely do not have to focus on. For example, we have only just started sales to South America, the monitor division is in the middle of a reorganisation and the netcast is too new to judge. Nobody obliges us to look at everything; in fact, time pressure more or less forces us to focus. Thoroughness is more of a weakness than a virtue.

Identify every part of the question that is not relevant – anything that has already been decided is insignificant or already completely clear. Then we no longer have to investigate those regions, product groups or distribution channels. What remains is the focus. Make sure that the data and financial figures that come to the fore are related to the main focus.

Step 2   Dissect the company's financial performance

You cannot investigate every aspect of the business in three months and that is not necessary. We focus on the areas that offer the most substantial and most likely opportunities to create value. To get a clearer view we first dissect the financial results. What is doing well and what is not looking so good? Don't just go along with what the financial director says – use an earnings tree.

An earnings tree breaks down the financial results (for example, the return on investment or the value creation) into their relevant commercial and operational parameters (such as the capital invested or the gross margin). The Du Pont tree is still the best-known tree. An earnings tree does not look the same for every business sector. The points that are important for capital intensive sectors, for example, are different from those that are of importance in the service sector. Choose the most promising parameters when constructing your own tree, but make sure that it is arithmetically correct; do not leave any parameters out of the formula.

We'll use a chain of fashion stores as an example. The return on investment (ROI) needs to increase, but in three months we cannot fully investigate turnover, margins, costs and capital invested. Therefore we first draw up an earnings tree, in this case a simple ROI tree (see Figure 1.1).

The earnings tree offers a first insight into how the various parts of the fashion chain perform, but it is not easy to reach a conclusion. That an ROI of 5% is not very good can be gleaned from the capital market, but it is not clear whether a turnover of €2550 per square metre of shop floor is good or bad. We therefore need a broader context. Choose one of two ways to achieve this.

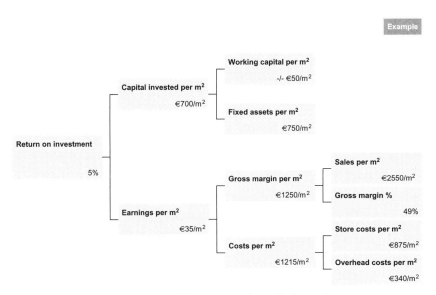

Example

Figure 1.1 A simple ROI tree for a fashion chain

Compare with competitors ('differences')

If comparable competitors obtain a noticeably larger turnover or margin per square metre, the problem is obvious. The investigation must focus seriously on sales. We do not of course know all the financial details of our competitors, but by using an annual report and making some educated guesses we can usually find out quite a lot.

Compare with the past ('changes')

If the fashion chain previously achieved a greater turnover or profit margin per square metre of shop floor, that is a clear sign. There may still be all sorts of other things going on, but the sales capability must in any case be investigated.

A comparative earnings tree for a fashion chain can look like Figures 1.2 and 1.3. The earnings tree shows that our fashion chain has a commercial problem. Things seem to be going particularly wrong at the level of the retail outlet.

The problem is not with the locations or the company's image and name recognition, as is shown by the number of visitors. The conversion from visitor to customer seems to be in line with competition. However, average transaction value falls behind. The product range, the service and the store layout must therefore be investigated further. This is good to know later on when we formulate the central question.

We can of course also draw up an earnings tree per region, per division, etc. The less homogeneous the company, the more you will want to break down the results. A company that is present in a number of different countries with various different product divisions requires a more detailed earnings tree than a national company with a single set of products.

Step 3   Be mindful of changes in the market

Important changes in the market offer a further starting point for the central question. Changes can present a problem but they can also offer opportunities, for example for new value creation.

How do we react to 'business sector revolutions'? A business sector is sometimes 'shaken up' because clients radically alter their purchasing behaviour or because innovative technology creates new opportunities. We do not want to define such

Comparative ROI tree

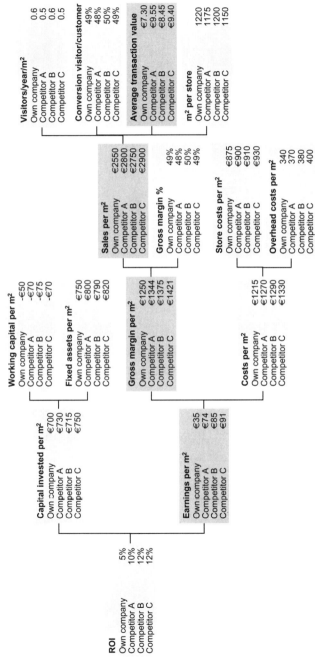

Figure 1.2 Comparisons with competitors reveal the problem

Comparative ROI tree

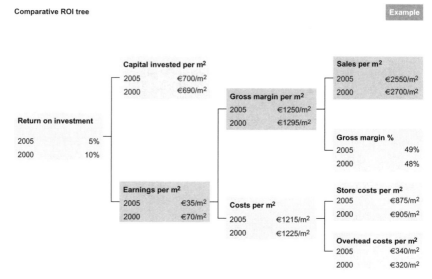

Figure 1.3 Comparisons with the past also reveal the problem

changes out of the content of the question. That would be like optimising the company of the past.

You don't have to invent the steam engine in order to shake up a business sector. Less dramatic developments can also cause revolutions. Just to mention a couple of examples from the recent past:

- *Low cost airlines* offer their customers 'stripped down' services, where extras must be paid for separately, where only individual point-to-point connections are made available, often at secondary airports, and where tickets can no longer be altered. This came as a shock to an industry that up to then had mainly competed on the basis of customer service – which indeed was the key criterion for the choice of *airline of the year* – and on the basis of the size of the airline's network. Ever since its creation, low cost has been the fastest growing market segment.

- *The Internet* has substantially shaken up the private investor market. Suddenly individuals could buy and sell shares for a fraction of the fees charged by regular banks. The procedure was also much more user-friendly. The banks saw large numbers of previously not very mobile clients deserting them for other providers.

There are no recipes for unexpected revolutions in business sectors; if there were, they wouldn't be unexpected. However, one can identify a number of situations that often accompany changes.

Commodity versus speciality

Where specialities turn into commodities, or vice versa, the heroes of yesteryear often become the marginal players of today. Thus, office automation (mainly hardware management) has in recent years become more and more of a commodity. The emphasis is shifting to cost control. In contrast, the drinks market for the youth sector is becoming increasingly one of specialities. Every lifestyle has its own drinks, which have punched great holes in the market share of beer, for instance.

Direct versus indirect distribution

To optimise the organisation's efficiency and cut out unnecessary intermediate steps, direct forms of distribution are emerging in various areas of business. Sellers and buyers alike are initiating this development. Insurers and hardware manufacturers are cutting out their middlemen, fashion labels are setting up their own retail outlets, and supermarkets are avoiding the wholesale sector by delivering straight to the stores themselves. But the opposite is also occurring. Companies are leaving their purchasing and stock control to specialised service providers or wholesalers who, through their specialised systems, their specific competencies and their economies of scale, can offer advantages in costs and quality.

Discount offers versus service

In business sectors where there is little difference between the various players, or sectors that have always delivered high quality services or products, space can sometimes open up for discount offers. These can make things very awkward for the established parties, through the use of a different business model or a different offer. See, for example, the low cost airlines mentioned above.

Specialisation versus integration

One example of specialisation is the temping agency. Specialised employment agencies are created, which concentrate on specific sectors of industry and business, to which they deliver appropriately qualified personnel. The 'broad-based' agencies also develop particular approaches for specific sectors. An example of integration in services is facility management.

Services such as cleaning, security, reception and catering services, which clearly have much ground in common, are combined by facility managers to create an integrated package of services. This can have operational advantages, but also commercial gains if it means client contacts are better utilised.

Regulation versus deregulation

Market changes may also be a result of changes in legislation, such as deregulation and privatisation or the removal of trade barriers, or, conversely, they may arise from stronger regulation in areas such as security and the environment.

A well-known framework with which to measure the attractiveness of a business sector is Porter's five forces model. The model gives a very useful rundown of the five forces that together determine whether anything can be earned in a business sector: the threat of substitutes, buyer power, supplier power, the threat of entry and the intensity of rivalry. A change in one of these forces can affect the attractiveness of the business sector, but also the competitive position of the company. The five forces model is very easy to use and elicits fundamental questions: 'Do we really want to remain active in this sector, and if so, in what capacity?'

Step 4 Watch what competitors are doing

It goes without saying that we always keep an eye on the competition, on their product line, their prices, their

availability, etc. We react by adjusting our prices where necessary, by launching new products or by negotiating with the
distribution channels. The total amount of information about
the competition is too great for us to look at it all in detail. We
focus on the most influential competitors, such as our most
important direct competitors and on so-called 'outsiders' in
the sector, who, for example, introduce new technological
developments. With our strategy formulation process we can
look at our competitors from a number of angles.

Look at the competitor 'top-down' from a financial point of view

Try to put together an earnings tree for a number of prominent competitors (see above). Using this we can distinguish
areas where we should be able to do better.

Think about the meaning of 'inexplicable' behaviour

Sometimes the competitor demonstrates behaviour that we
cannot explain from our own personal point of view. Has
the competitor gone mad? Naturally, the competitor is not
always right, but sometimes you can learn a lot from such
observations. Ask the sales staff about signs such as the
following:

• The competitor offers a product for sale at a price that is
  even lower than our own manufacturing costs. Does the
  competitor have a smarter production process? Are we in

the process of pricing ourselves out of the market due to a faulty cost allocation system?

- The competitor performs very successfully but we rarely come across him in the market: has our competitor entered new markets? Has he successfully expanded or shifted his market?

- We experience rapid growth in a specific client segment, which our competitor appears to have abandoned. Are we pulling in the unattractive customers, for instance as a result of an incorrect cost allocation or weakness in our pricing policy?

- The competitor has introduced discounts, although we know that the client is most interested in service and added value. Has the purchasing behaviour of the client changed without our having noticed?

Talk to clients, especially those of the competitor

It is of course important to serve your own clients as well as possible, but in order to grow it is perhaps even more important to start serving well precisely those who are your competitors' clients. Conversations with your own clients can raise very useful points, but conversations with non-clients not infrequently reveal startling insights. See whether you can speak to a non-client today by approaching one who has recently left you or by phoning someone who has rejected an offer from you.

Step 5 Formulate the central question

From the first four steps a clear picture should have emerged of the company's real concerns. If the concerns are connected, we incorporate them into one central problem. If not, then we have to choose just one of the separate paths. We convert the central problem into a question – the question, the central question. This is the basis for the issue tree and the work plan that we are going to develop in this phase. It is this central question that we will attempt to answer through this project.

Make sure that you have a sufficiently specific central question (see Figure 1.4). Frequently asked questions such as: 'Where do we as a company want to be in five years' time?' or: 'What kind of company do we want to be?' do not give the

Characteristics of the central question

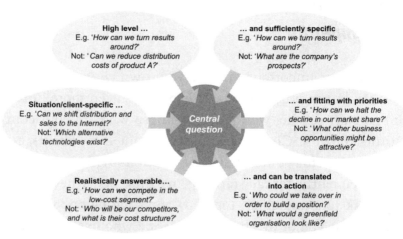

Figure 1.4 A usable central question fulfils a number of requirements

team anything concrete to work on. Try to make the question more specific. Ask, for example: 'Do we need to review our distribution in the light of the rise of *direct writers*, and if so, how?' or: 'Is it an attractive idea to expand into Scandinavia, and should this be carried out by our own organisation, through agents, through takeovers or by other means?'

The degree of urgency determines whether the central question is awkward to find:

- Acute problems require a prompt solution. In such cases you do not usually need to philosophise at great length about the substance of the central question.

- Underperformance compared with the past or with competitors indicates that things can be done better, without it being a case of acute urgency. Getting to the bottom of such concerns demands a bit more detective work.

- The most difficult thing is to identify concerns about future performance, especially if no problem is yet visible. Who can say how the company should be equipped so that it will also perform well in the future? It is, however, precisely this type of question that we want to raise in the strategy project.

At this stage the central question is at most a 'best guess' and not yet definitive. This week, but also during the analysis phase, there will be room enough to adapt and refine the question.

Step 6 Test the central question with senior management

It is obvious that you should involve in particular the company's senior management in formulating the key question. We have two goals here.

Testing

We can expect the directors of the company to have the 'big questions' on their minds – who else would? Does the central question as we have formulated it get to the core of the matter? Does our question fit in with the company's priorities? Are there any significant changes to be made to the central question, from the point of view of senior managers? Does senior management have anything relevant to add?

Building commitment

If the directors of the organisation do not find our question and this process important, the answer will also not be important. In this case making a major effort (for that is what it is!) to find that answer is misplaced. Therefore, right from the start of the process we need to have a prominent position on the company leadership's agenda. This project must become an important project. If not, then it must not become a project at all.

A brief discussion is in many cases somewhat inadequate for this purpose. Many people can no longer stand to hear the term 'brainstorming session', but a comprehensive workshop is the best idea. It won't be easy to free up the top management for a lengthy session at such short notice. If you do succeed, it is worth taking the trouble to prepare such a session very thoroughly.

Those who have been doing all the thinking up to this point do not, incidentally, have to adopt too docile an attitude during such a session. The central question has been given a lot of thought; assume that it is not a load of nonsense. Be sure not to let yourself be blown over by the first little sigh of a verbal headwind. Be firm and have trust in the initial analyses in defending your central question. Keep your eyes open for possible objections to the project, conflicting agendas, hobbyhorses, pet projects and power struggles within the organisation.

Use this session as well to get to know senior management's expectations in a wider sense. What sort of end product do they have in mind? How will they measure the success of this project? How much time is available for the project and how is the top management thinking of dividing up the total time? In what way and to what extent does senior management wish to contribute to the project? In short, everything that you come across in this book regarding the strategy process.

2

Days 6 and 7 – We set up a project organisation

What is the goal for these days?

Why does thinking freely on your own about a broad subject, without any time pressure or responsibility, so seldom lead to usable results? Few people have the gift of combining creativity, logic and discipline into a well-argued strategic document, delivered on time. Even at a consultancy organisation the most productive advisor might be seen wandering around for days with a 'where shall I start' expression, if he is working alone on a task. Even one week later he may only have produced a pile of scrap paper covered in arrows and squiggles. Is this because we need argument in order to refine our ideas? Do we gain energy from a team?

Whatever the case may be, formulating strategy means team-work. A well-briefed team under time pressure can work wonders. The team members stimulate one another's creativity, test one another's logic and pool their combined experience to create a heady mixture. Their productivity and creativity would be unthinkable without the adrenaline boost that a team provides. An effective strategy project in a team can be the highpoint of someone's career. In such an environment ideas are formed and friendships are forged.

The team must be bedded into a clear project structure (Figure 2.1) in order to ensure sufficient progress and to monitor quality. What steps do we take today?

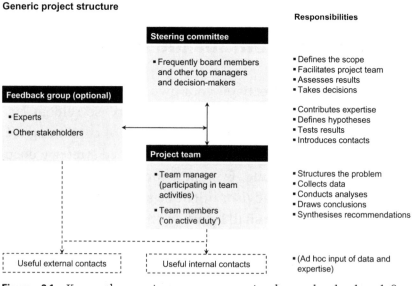

Figure 2.1 Keep the project structure simple and clearly define responsibilities

Step 1   Choose appropriate team members

The initial tendency of those who put together a strategy team is to bring together the most experienced line managers. After all, they know the company best and won't talk rubbish. Why is this a bad idea? First, these people have no time. Perhaps they think they have time, saying: 'I'll clear my diary and then I can devote two days a week to the project.' Unfortunately this never works. Second, line managers are often burdened by the past. They have a tendency to want to prove that 'it wasn't their fault'. The various parties usually end up by agreeing that it was nobody's fault but this takes up a lot of time and energy. Third, line managers are not always so keen on all kinds of mathematical puzzles. They often don't want to get involved in such things ('I'm not going to sit in front of a spreadsheet).

The second tendency is to select people who just happen to have nothing to do at that particular moment. This is also a bad idea. They do have time but their suitability is a matter of chance. Once the smoke from the selection process has cleared, it often reveals a team comprising the 'hard to place' members of the organisation. Are they going to determine the future of the organisation?

In the team members we look for a mix of promising, ambitious colleagues, together with a number of specialists in the relevant fields. Their role in the team can be a way of involving them more strongly in the management of the company, as a preparation for later stages in their career. The team members must have a number of characteristics in common:

- They have proven analytical and quantitative skills and are preferably also good with spreadsheets and databases.

- They have enough time for the project. Try to ensure that the team members are available for four or five days a week. If availability is lower than three days per week the team's efficiency declines rapidly.

- They have a marked desire to achieve results, even if the analysis is not yet complete in every detail.

- They are good team players. One highly talented eccentric can be kept in check, but having several loose cannon in the team quickly lays too great a strain on the team manager.

The ideal team member is an intelligent, driven, middle manager or functionary who has already built up a certain network and who preferably has clear potential to make progress within the company. Make sure that such a team member has something to gain from being part of the team. An ambitious member of staff can use the project to prove him or herself to senior management and at the same time gain a good knowledge of important issues. You often see members of such project groups again a few years later and find that they have been given considerable responsibilities.

Of course, not only must the individuals be suitable but the team as a whole must also 'gel'. Are the functional areas sufficiently represented, can a good contribution be expected from all the team members and do the team members get on well together?

Make sure that the people the intended team members report to agree with the make-up of the team; over the next three months the team members will not be spending much time in their own departments.

Make sure that you reach agreements with the line managers as to who directs the team members and how to divide their time between their regular work and the project.

Step 2   Forge a team

Separate team members do not yet constitute a team. Make sure that there is a well-understood set of team goals and that there are agreements on roles, procedures and ways of working together (see Figure 2.2).

Key elements of teamwork

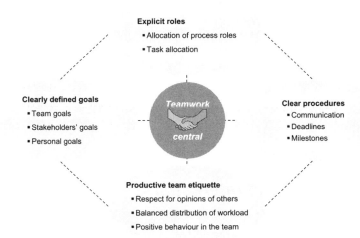

Figure 2.2   Team effectiveness depends on clarity of purpose and how to achieve it

Clear aims

What are we trying to achieve together over the coming weeks? What is the rough timescale that we are working with? And what individual aims might each of the team members have? Do they want to learn or demonstrate anything specific?

Clear roles

Although the precise tasks of the team are not yet clear at this stage, make sure that each team member knows the general contours of their role. What area of expertise have we been chosen for? What, roughly, is expected of us in the coming weeks? Where do the responsibilities lie within the team?

Clear procedures

How do we deal with potential deadlines? How do we communicate with one another? How do we manage our presence on the team, given the other responsibilities of each team member?

A mature way of interacting

How do we achieve a balanced division of labour? How do we stimulate a positive attitude in each team member and how do we go about discussing potential areas of conflict?

A strategy project is not a competition and colleagues are not competitors. Nurture a stimulating atmosphere. Give team members the chance to create this atmosphere; organise a team dinner in the first week and arrange some informal contact, preferably each week, even if it only means having pizza together in the team room. Encourage team members to work together in pairs. If two team members conduct interviews together, for example, this is not only useful but also a good way of getting to know each other.

Step 3   Create a dynamic climate

Whenever a project of this sort gets off the ground a large number of people in the company are usually only too ready to share their ideas (sometimes their hobbyhorses) with the team, to help determine the course of action and to comment on results. When it comes to doing the actual work, the queue of willing helpers suddenly shrinks dramatically. Everyone loves making comments, but real work is a very different matter. But work is what it boils down to: collecting data, sitting at the computer making spreadsheets, preparing presentations and so on. This is why a dynamic climate is necessary (see Figures 2.3 and 2.4). The comments and hobbyhorses will come of their own accord.

A dynamic climate in particular stimulates the achievement of end products. A task or an analysis must always provide an end product. The question of how we get to these end products comes later on, but whether an end product is in this case a (part of a) work plan, a well-documented insight or a (procedural) decision, every person

Eight characteristics of effective teams

1. High level of ambition

2. Strong 'can do' mentality

3. Common sense of urgency

4. Willingness to invest in each another

5. True commitment to team goals

6. Flexible, open attitude

7. Bilateral support and trust

8. Encouraging and fun atmosphere

Figure 2.3 Effective teams have recognisable characteristics

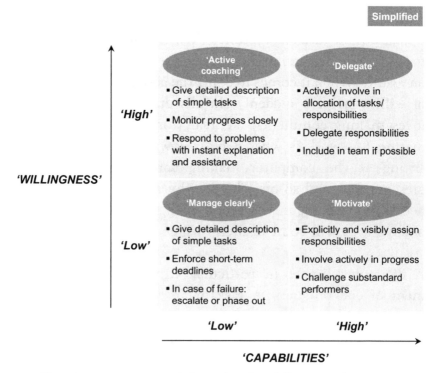

Figure 2.4 Management styles tailored to different work contacts

must continually ask themselves: 'What end product am I working on today?'

In consultancy firms the saying goes: *an end product a day keeps the manager away*. The end product is the tangible fruit of every effort or inspiration.

Step 4   Appoint a steering committee and possibly a feedback group

We are going to find something out, but for whom? There must be a committee that is capable of evaluating findings and that has the power to make decisions. This can be senior management or a section thereof, possibly with the addition of shareholder representatives or other stakeholders. In future we will refer to it as the steering committee.

In addition it might make sense to appoint a feedback group, if the problem is a complex one or if there are numerous interested parties. This group has no decision-making power, but it can warn about errors, side effects or conflicts of interest. Material must of course be examined first by the feedback group before it can be presented to the steering committee.

Step 5   Sort out the practicalities

At what junctures will the team report back? Plan a number of reporting times, such as the end of the first week in order to discuss the central question and work plans. This can be done with the chair of the steering committee on their own if there is no room in diaries at this time. Afterwards at least two further reporting sessions are needed: one near the end of the analysis phase, when there are all sorts of findings but no conclusions, and one at the end of the project, in order to present the conclusions. Between these reporting sessions the team manager consults regularly on an informal basis with the chair of the steering committee, in order to avoid major shocks and steer round pitfalls. Set these reporting dates now.

Without a team room, in which the team members can get together each day, the team will not become a unit. If the team members work each at their own desk, the project quickly acquires overtones of contract work: if I do these tasks for you, is that my lot then? There must be opportunities for collective joy in response to good ideas and shared concern if the team is stuck (see Figure 2.5).

Step 6   Get the ball rolling

A flying start requires a productive kick-off session, at which at least three parties are present. First of all invite the project initiators, often also members of the steering committee. Second, make sure that the team members are there at the kick-off as they are going to do the work, after all. Third, invite members of staff of whom we have something to expect during the project. These are the in-house data providers (the cost controller, the head of human resources, the marketing information officer) and the experts (the marketing manager, the production manager).

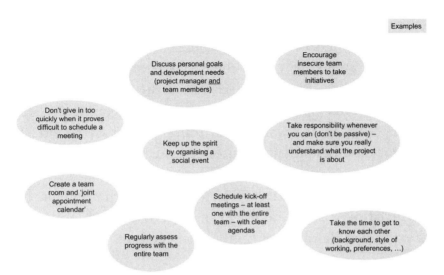

Examples

Discuss personal goals and development needs (project manager <u>and</u> team members)

Encourage insecure team members to take initiatives

Don't give in too quickly when it proves difficult to schedule a meeting

Take responsibility whenever you can (don't be passive) – and make sure you really understand what the project is about

Keep up the spirit by organising a social event

Create a team room and 'joint appointment calendar'

Schedule kick-off meetings – at least one with the entire team – with clear agendas

Take the time to get to know each other (background, style of working, preferences, ...)

Regularly assess progress with the entire team

Figure 2.5 There are a multitude of ways to avoid problems in the team

At the kick-off session we want to reach agreement on the central question, we want everyone to agree to cooperate and we want to make practical arrangements. The agenda for a kick-off session might look like this:

- Background, urgency and financial impact

- Goal and central question

- Initial outlines of a work plan (if available)

- Project organisation and responsibilities

- Practical matters (meetings diary, communication within the organisation, confidentiality, expected time commitment, etc.).

Once the team has made a start, the organisation is quick to realise that there is 'something going on'. The team members are more often absent from their regular workplace, all sorts of requests for information go round the organisation, the team room fills up with piles of paper and intriguing flipchart sheets hang on the walls. Such things do not go unnoticed and for this reason it is sensible to explain something about the project to the organisation, at least the goal and the overall timing. Middle managers of departments that might be involved need to be informed in more detail. After all, we want to be able to count on their cooperation.

3
Day 8 – We structure the question

What is the goal for this day?

On the first day we transformed a vague concern into a concrete central question which we formulated in a precise, clear and relevant fashion. However, this question is still very complex and must be approached in a number of different ways. Take, for example, the question: 'Is expansion into Scandinavia attractive and, if so, should this be achieved by our own organisation, through agents, through takeovers or by other methods?'

Deductive and inductive

Drawing up an issue tree requires a combination of deductive and inductive thinking.

A *deductive* line of reasoning means deriving the specific from the general. We derive specific conclusions from general truths. Deductive reasoning comes closest to what is meant by 'logical thinking'. Conclusions are derived from general facts or suppositions in an analytical–mathematical way, or main questions are split up into subsidiary questions. This method of reasoning, which is also needed for all sorts of model building and quantitative analysis, places demands particularly on a person's analytical skills. The outcome of deductive reasoning is an answer that can easily be judged objectively and verified. If all premises are true, then logically the answer must also be true.

An *inductive* line of reasoning means deriving the general from the specific. We develop generally valid theories from specific truths. Thus, for example, hypotheses are formed on the basis of a limited number of observations. This method of reasoning places demands in particular on conceptual skills, or, shall we say, creativity and experience. The outcome of inductive reasoning is a lot less 'hard and fast' than that of deductive reasoning. The observations and arguments collected make the reasoning acceptable, but do not constitute definite proof.

It takes quite a bit to answer this question. We need to know, for example, whether the Scandinavian market is attractive, whether our products are to the tastes of Scandinavian consumers – maybe we can develop products especially for this market – and what form of distribution is feasible and affordable.

We need to structure the central question before we can answer it efficiently and effectively. Today we are going to split the central question into bite-sized subsidiary questions. We call the result the *issue tree* (see Figure 3.1). Drawing up the issue tree is the goal of an important, comprehensive and substantial first session with the newly formed team. The issue tree forms the basis of the work plan and guides the team's thinking during these three months. The issue tree is also an important way for the team members to make the working methods their own and to allow them to get the hang of working together.

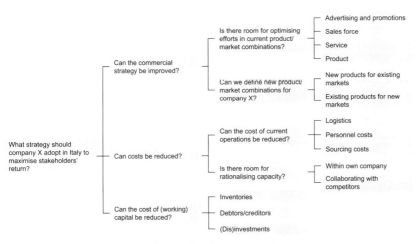

Figure 3.1   Example of a generic issue tree

Step 1   Make an inventory of the questions

We are going to sit down with the team and write down all the questions that occur to us to ask if we should want to answer the central question.

Work with a flipchart for preference, so that the whole team can join in. Do not worry at this stage about potential connections or overlap between questions. We first want to define the area of uncertainty. Pose some helpful questions as a team to get the thinking process going, such as:

- What functional areas are connected with the central question (marketing, product development, sales, production, distribution, transport, etc.) and what are the most important uncertainties in each functional area?

- What would we as an organisation have to do in order to achieve the ambition contained in the central question? If the central question is about expansion into Scandinavia, for example, think about everything that is involved in such an expansion and what the relevant questions are.

- Why do I suspect that the answer to the question will be positive or, alternatively, that it will be negative?

Make sure that the team produces real questions (see Figure 3.2). There is a tendency to write, for example, 'the market', although 'the market' is not a question. What do we want to know about the market exactly? What aspects of the market are decisive for the answer to the question? If, instead of asking concrete questions, we refer to all sorts of catchwords, aspects or areas of expertise, we are not doing our team any favours.

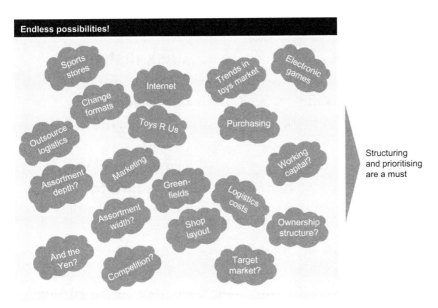

Examples

It is not about conducting analyses...

- Market size assessment
- Market growth assessment
- Competitor analyses
- Cost benchmarking
- Interviewing clients
- Financial modelling
- Assessment of business models
- ...

... but about answering strategic questions

- Which adjacent markets offer attractive growth opportunities?
- How can we strengthen our competitive position?
- Which accounts can we grow?
- What are the profit prospects of these activities?
- Which companies would be promising acquisition candidates?
- ...

Figure 3.2 What is the strategy team's role?

Endless possibilities!

Sports stores
Internet
Trends in toys market
Electronic games
Change formats
Toys R Us
Purchasing
Outsource logistics
Assortment depth?
Marketing
Green-fields
Working capital?
Logistics costs
Assortment width?
Shop layout
Ownership structure?
And the Yen?
Competition?
Target market?

Structuring and prioritising are a must

Figure 3.3 Practical questions instead of sound bites

We increase the amount of work involved rather than reducing it. Of course there is an infinite amount to find out and to tell about 'the market', which can never be covered in three months. It is only by posing concrete subsidiary questions in a recognisable question form that we create more focus and make the central question easier to solve (see Figure 3.3).

Next, ensure that questions are posed in such a way that each answer elicits a conclusion. Do not ask: 'How big is the market?' because the answer will be a figure, which will not show directly whether the market can be considered to be large or small. This subsidiary question does not elicit any conclusion. Ask rather: 'Is the market attractive?' This question elicits an answer that is relevant to our ambition of expanding into Scandinavia: 'Yes, the Scandinavian market has relatively attractive price levels and its volume is higher than that of our home market.'

Don't ask . . .	**. . . ask instead**
How large is the Scandinavian market?	Is the Scandinavian market attractive?
What is the market structure in Scandinavia?	Given the Scandinavian market structure, is there room for a wholesaler?
How high are production costs in Scandinavia?	Are production costs in Scandinavia significantly lower than in our current locations?
What are our working capital needs?	Can working capital be reduced?

At the end of this first team session the wall of the team room is hung with a large number of questions: the 'shopping list'.

It's a good start but it is not yet a usable end product for today.

Step 2   Choose a structure for the issue tree

A 'shopping list' of questions is not yet an issue tree. First, not every question on the list is equally suitable as a subsidiary question in the issue tree. Each subsidiary question must determine part of the answer. If it does not, we can save ourselves trouble by leaving out those questions that are not relevant. Second, it is not productive to use questions that overlap too much as that only doubles the workload. We do want to see a comprehensive issue tree as we might otherwise reach the wrong conclusions. If the answers to all of our subsidiary questions support expansion into Scandinavia and we come to the conclusion later on that expansion into Scandinavia is not a good idea, then our issue tree must have been incomplete.

Third, such a 'shopping list' does not indicate any links between the various questions. Are they ranked in a hierarchical relationship or are they of equal value? In other words, can you answer one question by finding the answers to a number of subsidiary questions or does each question stand alone and demand the same amount of attention? We must bring structure to the shopping list of questions so that the problem becomes manageable.

Our approach is strongly influenced by the structure of the issue tree but the choice of a structure for the issue tree is strongly driven by our prior knowledge. Someone who does not yet have any background knowledge about the question under investigation is more likely to draw up a purely analytical, generic issue tree structure. We split the problem into sections, such as turnover, costs and investment, or the domestic market and the export side. Someone who has a better idea of where the rub is can create a more substantial and specific issue tree structure. In this case we identify in the subsidiary questions the areas that we know to be most critical for the future. Someone who has even more insight into the question, or who already has concrete hypotheses, can even ask very specific subsidiary questions.

The general rule is that the more specific the issue tree, the easier it is to answer the question. As the issue tree becomes more specific, the parts of the universe that do not have to be investigated become ever larger and the project becomes less labour intensive. For this reason, try to be as specific as possible. After all, our goal is not to investigate all aspects of the question; our goal is to find an answer to the central question.

If necessary, each of the subsidiary questions can be divided further into sub-subsidiary questions. Be practical in doing this as it only makes sense to split questions if it makes those questions easier to answer. A theoretically correct division, which the team cannot deal with in practice, makes little sense. Above all, do not strive for symmetry. If one subsidiary question is subdivided, it does not automatically mean that another question must also be split. Another point: do not try to make the issue tree too attractive by avoiding overlaps between questions at all costs. A certain amount of overlap can easily be managed and does not cause any problems. Here the rule also applies that an issue tree is not a museum exhibit, it is purely a tool.

Example: issue trees

Say the central question is whether a particular ferry service can be made profitable. Someone who knows little about this ferry service and who has to solve this problem will draw up a fairly *analytical, generic* issue tree. They will, for example, identify in the subsidiary questions each of the various aspects of the company's earnings. The central question is whether the ferry service's financial result can be improved. Subsidiary questions could then be:

- Can income be increased?

- Can costs be reduced?

- Can working capital be reduced?

Someone who has looked more closely at ferry services will have a better idea of what determines the earnings of a ferry service. Using this knowledge, a *more insightful, more substantial and specific* (but still general) issue tree can be developed, for example:

- Can income from ticket sales be improved by applying yield-management techniques or by offering higher value transport solutions?

- Can onboard sales be intensified by professionalising the retail sales activities, possibly with the help of partners?

- Can the size of the fleet be reduced by drawing up a more efficient sailing schedule?

This version already makes it possible to carry out a more precisely targeted investigation. However, someone who knows this particular ferry service well will know even better which factors determine the company's results. Thus, *an even more specific* issue tree can be drawn up:

- Can the ferry service compete with the newly opened bridge by offering other services, such as fast hydrofoil connections to more distant destinations, with appropriate fares in the holiday season?

- Is the existing retailer ready and able to provide onboard catering and retail sales services, under attractive conditions, in addition to their onshore activities?

- Can the size of the fleet be reduced by swapping capacity between commuter ferry services (especially at peak times) and freight services (especially after the arrival of intercontinental container ships)?

Step 3 Test the issue tree against a number of criteria

Finally, take a look at what the team has produced and test it against a number of simple criteria.

Is the issue tree complete?

Have all relevant subsidiary questions been asked? Do all the key aspects of the central question appear in subsidiary questions? Have any aspects been overlooked? It is a rule here that the more analytical the issue tree, the easier it is to check whether it is complete. If you cut the question analytically into a number of sections, you can usually establish with a high degree of certainty whether the parts add up to the whole. After all, if you have added up turnover, costs and capital, or if you have added up domestic turnover and export, nothing remains. The more specific the issue tree, the harder it is to check this. More thought is needed to work out whether any important aspects have been overlooked.

Is the issue tree not too complete?

Do we need an answer to every subsidiary question to be able to answer the central question? Why are we looking for this particular fact or this insight? Do we really need this insight and is it crucial to finding an answer to the central question? Scrap any unnecessary questions on the issue tree as this will save time and effort.

Do the questions lead to a definite answer? Are there still any questions of the 'how big is the market?' sort? For each question imagine a hypothetical answer and ask yourself whether it is good or bad, whether it elicits a positive or a negative answer to the central question. Say the answer to a particular subsidiary question is '42'. What does that tell us?

Are the questions linked to practical, feasible steps to be taken?

However sensible a subsidiary question might be in theory, it is of no use if it doesn't help you to think of any practical follow-up steps. If you want to go to Scandinavia you can ask yourself whether there are other possible obstacles standing in the way of your company exporting to that region. This may be very relevant, but what do you do with such a question? It encompasses potential technical, commercial and legal aspects, and possibly others as well, but where do you start? Anyone who is landed with this subsidiary question will probably be very unhappy and will in any case be extremely busy.

Is it possible to make the issue tree even more specific?

Structuring is an ongoing process. We must continually check whether we can make the structure even more specific. This can be risky (see above) but it does result in a more focused work plan.

4

Day 9 – We formulate hypotheses

What is the goal for this day?

At the end of the third day we drew up an issue tree as a basis for a work plan for the following weeks. If all went well, we managed with this issue tree to pinpoint the most relevant aspects of the central question. That will already save us some effort, but we have one more method at our disposal to save ourselves more work. That is to formulate strong *hypotheses*. If we have a strong hypothesis for a particular subsidiary question we do not need to answer the question in its entirety. To start with we can simply test the hypothesis. Only if the hypothesis turns out to be wrong do we have to search for another answer. By using hypotheses we can work in a much more targeted way. Hypotheses strengthen the focus of our analyses. Today's goal is to determine whether we can formulate strong hypotheses for particular subsidiary questions and, if so, what these hypotheses are. What steps do we take today?

Step 1   Look for possible hypotheses

Formulating hypotheses is a purely inductive process. It demands a reasonable knowledge of the company and the business sector, and it requires a certain creativity. There is no inescapable logic that unerringly leads to usable hypotheses. It is a matter of trial and error.

A usable hypothesis can be tested (otherwise you can never reject it), is specific enough (just like the questions) and is targeted at a solution (otherwise it is of no use to us). A purely descriptive hypothesis such as 'Price levels in Scandinavia are relatively low' is not wrong, but a more usable version would be 'Our production costs are too high to be able to compete in the Scandinavian market'. Better still is 'We have to produce in a different way in order to compete in the Scandinavian market'. The hypothesis 'We can compete on price in Scandinavia if we manufacture in China' is even more precisely targeted at a conclusion. Just as with the development of the issue tree, the rule is that if the hypothesis is more specific, the task will be less labour intensive but riskier.

It is possible that certain hypotheses have already emerged over the last few days. The formulation of the central question and the development of an issue tree in particular are a fruitful source of hypotheses. In addition, use internal sources to generate new hypotheses.

Interview a number of key people in the organisation, as they can be valuable providers of hypotheses. But remain critical.

Beware of anecdotes

The sales department in particular tends to generate quite a bit of anecdotal material that lends itself well to the creation of strong hypotheses. The sales reps say, for example, that our clients find our product too expensive (but they are our clients so they apparently do buy the product), that there are a lot of complaints from clients (if clients do not complain more than they apparently do you have to ask yourself whether we are not perhaps making the product too attractive; the question is what section of the customer base is complaining and whether this is hitting turnover), or that we must advertise more (does the cost of advertising generate at least as much in profit margin?). Be critical.

Beware of moaning minnies

In the hypothesis stage key people have the tendency to indulge in general moaning. Although general complaints may well contain a grain of truth, they are seldom a good basis for hypotheses. Examples of common moans that are not specific enough to be used as hypotheses are:

- 'This management has no vision. We must develop a vision and be allowed to make choices.'

- 'This organisation is not fighting fit. We are not well enough prepared to compete.'

- 'We have the wrong mentality. We need a change of culture.'

- 'We are too inward-looking. We must act more with a view to our customers.'

- 'Political games are destroying this company. Everyone here has their own little fiefdom.'

Watch out for 'passing the buck'

Both head office staff and line management can deliver exciting hypotheses. Line managers often have more detailed knowledge of the business but they are sometimes more concerned with making themselves look good, as in 'It's not our fault – it's those guys from that other department who don't have a clue'. Avoid the question of who is to blame for what and aim to keep an open mind towards your interlocutors.

Force yourselves to answer subsidiary questions as a team. One technique for obtaining a team answer is to write the subsidiary questions on separate sheets of paper and hang them on the wall of the team room. Each team member writes their own 'best answer', supported by arguments, for example on self-adhesive notes, and sticks it to the appropriate sheet. Each piece of paper thus ends up with a number of independent answers to a question on it, with the motives behind the answer. The team can then use the answers to stimulate a discussion on each question.

Step 2   Make a selection from the hypotheses

Not every hypothesis is equally plausible. Even hypotheses put forward by senior management are not necessarily true. Remain critical. Only venture forth with really believable hypotheses and even then be careful. Subject the hypotheses to a first test:

- Is the hypothesis an answer to a question in our issue tree? If not, the hypothesis is superfluous, whether true or false. After all, the issue tree provided all the relevant questions. Or was the issue tree apparently still not complete?

- Does the hypothesis agree with our initial observations, for example with the facts from our results tree? If the hypothesis does not square with these facts there is no need for further tests.

In many cases it is sensible not to inform the organisation about the hypotheses yet. Hypotheses can be a burden for particular employees; why spread panic with hypotheses that have not yet been tested?

5

Day 10 – We make a work plan

What is the goal for this day?

There are relevant questions, maybe even hypotheses, but that still doesn't make a work plan. How are we going to answer the questions, which aspects of the company are we going to look at, who is going to do it and when will it be finished? Those are the elements of the work plan (see Figure 5.1) that we are going to create today. What are the possible steps?

A question is not an analysis. A question has an answer that fits, although it is not automatically clear how that answer must be reached. An analysis is an activity to which a concrete end product belongs, without it being automatically clear that this answers the question. The trick is to carry out

Issue	Sub-issue	Analyses/end products	Sources	Example Who?
The e-travel proposition is a good idea ...	As a product, travel is very suitable for e-commerce applications	Overview of the travel purchase process and the benefits of e-commerce in this process	Market research, industry association reports, internal and external interviews, Forrester	AW
		Actual development and projection of future online travel vs other online products	Forrester, press clippings, annual reports	AW
	As is illustrated by the many successful initiatives in this field abroad	Overview and (sales) development of international initiatives (and their characteristics)	Internet search, Forrester, annual reports, press clippings.	AW
	Domestic market is underdeveloped	Overview of domestic players' initiatives and their flaws	Internet search, press clippings	AW
... but it isn't focused enough as it stands ...	There are clearly distinct categories of travellers ...	Segmentation of travellers, including segment characteristics and sales	National Tourism Board, National Bureau of Statistics, etc.	BB
	... with different needs that are not easily met through one single proposition ...	Needs (offer, purchase process, content etc.) for each segment	Common sense	BB
	... as is shown by the offline operation	Linking traveller type to offline sales channel	Common sense + external interviews	BB
... and the logic behind it isn't always evident	Up-to-date content and street planner are irrelevant for consumers' decision-making, while the design lacks tourism content (which is important for consumers)	Overview of currently provided and missing content, and their role in the consumer's decision-making	Common sense, websites of competitors, interviews with travel agents (including National Railways travel agency)	BB
	Subscription fee for content which can be obtained free of charge elsewhere appears unrealistic	Overview of sources already offering up-to-date content free of charge	Internet search	CB
		Examples of other failed propositions charging for content	Press clippings, Internet	CB

Figure 5.1 Structured work plan to tackle project questions (hypothesis driven)

a number of analyses for each question, which allow us to find an answer.

Think of what you want to know in order to find a good answer to the question and formulate this as an analysis. This is not scientific research; above all keep things practical and concrete.

It has already been said earlier in this preparation phase that the analyses that need to be carried out depend on the questions that the team has asked itself, and the questions in turn depend on what we have defined as the central problem. No two strategy formulation processes are the same, however similar some situations may be. In short, a standardised list of analyses does not exist. However, we suggest below some possible types of analyses.

Step 1A   Design analyses for the questions – understanding customer behaviour

It says in every management book that it is important to have a good understanding of the customer. Unfortunately it is not so easy to build up such an understanding. Some activities may be considered as part of a three-month strategy project.

You can gain an overview of the customer's purchasing behaviour through interviews, questionnaires or focus groups with clients, or through a few good sessions together with your own sales staff. Who buys what, why and how? This gives us insight into three things.

The buying process

What steps does the buying process involve, which parties play a role, when can we as supplier try to influence whom? This is important for establishing our sales procedure, for selecting partners and wholesalers, etc.

The most important decision-maker

Who is the most important decision-maker, and about what? This tells us whom we must reach with our marketing and sales activities. This can have real strategic implications.

Purchasing criteria

On what basis is a purchasing decision made? This could be essential information for the team. What is needed in order to be successful in a particular client segment? How can we fulfil these requirements?

The mediocrity of the average

Anyone who wishes to gain insight into a particular company asks for figures and is given averages. The average turnover per client, the average margin, etc. The following example shows why this does not work: an employment agency's financial result is (too) modest. The average costs of serving a client are equal to the average gross margin. If you base yourself on these averages you come to the conclusion that there is no point in further increasing turnover – we still won't earn anything. But if you 'de-average' the client base you reveal some very attractive but also some very shaky client segments. At the individual client level the differences are even more pronounced. Only by getting away from averages can we carry out a targeted search for the real engines of profit.

In business-to-business environments, modelling the client economics is key, in order to understand what the possible price range is. The price range is determined by the costs of alternatives and the cost structure in the supply chain. We therefore do the following.

Map out the costs of alternatives to our product or to our service to the customer

It is not a case here of the costs that are theoretically relevant, but rather the costs included by the customer in their deliberations. Does the customer look only at the direct purchasing costs or do they also consider the costs of distribution (costs that are affected in other stages of the distribution chain) and life cycle costs (cost elements other than purchasing costs, such as maintenance costs, energy use and residual value)?

Map out the total cost structure and margin structure of the customer

The price range is partly determined by the costs of our product or service in relation to the client's margin.

Step 1B   Design analyses for the questions – understanding the market

In order to answer the questions in the issue tree, the team will in many cases want to know through what channels which customers consume what volume of products and how this changes over time. The following analyses are possible here.

Map out the market structure

How does volume 'travel' to the customer? How much volume is transferred via wholesalers, middlemen or the retailer sector to what sort of customers? What significance do imports and exports have and does the market also have captive parties?

Divide the market into segments where necessary. In the introduction we presented the market as a game that a company had to win. The strategist seeks out which game we can win and how. But most companies do not play just one game – they play many more. They serve different types of clients with different types of services and thus play in different markets. We must think about these separate markets and their playing rules if we are to think sensibly about our strategy. An average strategy for the average customer in the average market does not work.

Define volumes

As soon as you have chosen the relevant market and segmented it, it is often desirable to know how much volume is traded in each market. A *value map* is a practical way of showing the size of the various segments (see Figure 5.2).

Predict market growth

The attractiveness of many business sectors depends on market growth. Where the market is growing there is something to divide up; see Porter, who says that rivalry in a business sector – one of the five forces – is partly determined by growth.

Breakdown of new car sales, 2003
(No. of cars)

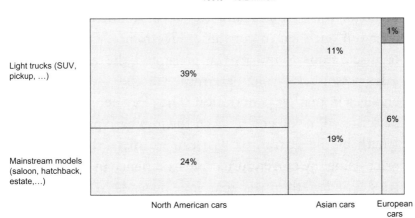

Figure 5.2 Only very few Americans buy European SUVs

Sensible predictions

How does the market develop? What are competitors going to do? Sooner or later in the development of a strategy predictions are on the agenda. The 'hockey stick curves' of the optimists are notorious. However, possibly more dangerous – because at first sight they look realistic – are those predictions that 'blindly' project developments from the past into the future. So how can you take a sensible peek into the future?

The recipe for a good prediction is to identify the drivers (price, volume, etc.) and estimate future development for each engine as well as possible. Let us look, for instance, at the sale of extended guarantees – often sold with consumer electronics. The drivers here are the number of appliances sold, the percentage of appliances for which an extended guarantee is given (penetration) and the average price per guarantee. For the number of appliances to be sold in future we can look, for example, at current sales, demographic changes and trends in countries that are ahead of our own in consumer electronics. On the basis of discussions found in the press and the estimates of sales personnel we can determine whether we can expect changes in market penetration. The price per guarantee is determined in the end by both the purchase price and the length of the guarantee. We can estimate the purchase price using the current price and experience in other countries. The length of the guarantee depends in this case to a great extent on international rulings. For this we could, for example, use two separate scenarios. All the drivers combined will then give us a prediction for the market as a whole. Pay most attention to the drivers that have most influence on the end result and where there is the greatest likelihood that they will change over the next few years.

There is a popular notion that there is no point in making predictions. The reasoning goes that as predictions never come true you must above all be flexible so as to react quickly to changes. Defenders of this way of thinking then point to all kinds of hockey stick curves (see box) and dubious extrapolations. This viewpoint saves a lot of work, but it is generally nonsense. Trying to make very precise predictions is indeed unlikely to be successful, but that does not excuse us in many cases from making a sensible and well-founded attempt to look at the future.

Step 1C   Design analyses for the questions – modelling the business economics

You often come across strategic plans containing the most wonderful proposals for products that we are going to make, customers that we are going to serve, new markets that we are going to enter, takeovers that we are going to carry out, without a single figure to show what such things cost and whether it is possible to make a profit with these plans. A strategy takes account of *business economics*. What does it cost and what does it deliver? Business economics are always a matter for discussion; only the way in which they are discussed varies in each case. One option is to model the cost structure.

Determine the relevant cost base

Which costs must be considered depends on the strategic question that we are trying to answer. Someone who wants to know whether they can profitably carry out a one-off order will make his calculations on the basis of the marginal costs. Someone struggling with the question of whether to close the factory will use the integral costs, but on the basis of the market value of assets, not on the basis of the original purchase price. In both cases the information we get from the controller or from the accountant does not suffice. That is already one important observation in relation to this analysis: standardised cost reporting is *hardly ever sufficient* for strategic analyses. The relevant cost basis is completely determined by the decision that we have to make. What costs do we avoid by giving up this client, this order, this service, this channel or this product? Those are the *avoidable* costs. Define which types of costs are completely or partly avoidable in the question that we have to answer.

Identify what drives costs

Here we have to quantify the chosen cost basis. Which costs are driven by what? For example, to what extent do the costs of sales depend on the number of customers, the number of incoming orders, the volume sold or the size of the product range? Which costs are 'fixed' and thus disappear only when one withdraws from the business sector? This is explicitly not a question of where the costs can be *allocated*. Cost allocations are the business of the accountant and we are concerned with the strategy. In our case it is a question of how the costs vary in the real world under the influence of particular decisions within the company.

Model the costs

Look only at the relevant costs and bear in mind the segmentation that we decided on. Work out the cost structure for each segment but possibly also per product or per channel, insofar as these are not yet part of the segmentation.

You must realise that costs vary each year as a result of changes in the costs of various factors (labour, energy) and improvements in productivity. The question remains to what extent this should be included in the cost calculations. In all likelihood competitors will see their factor costs change and their productivity improve in roughly the same measure. It only makes sense to spend much time on this issue if there are structural differences between the various parties, such as different production processes with other factor costs.

Look for opportunities in the area of costs

Now that we understand the costs we can start to play around with them. If there are considerable economies of scale (economies of scale are often exaggerated, see box) we must work out how to create scale. If there are important costs linked to complexity, for example because of the size of the range, we must consider whether a more modest range might not also suffice.

If we do not want to touch the cost structure, another possibility is to expose the price mechanism. In some cases we can work out quite precisely how the market price comes about and even how it will develop further. We can get quite far with these kinds of analyses, especially in the commodity business sector.

The supply curve: an analytical instrument for commodity business sectors

Differentiation or cost leadership, says Porter. It pretty much automatically comes down to the second option for organisations that produce a commodity. The customer has no real preference as regards the supplier so price is the criterion that determines choice. In such markets companies aim to achieve the lowest possible cost price. The company that has a lower cost price than its competitor can earn more with the same market price. A company whose cost price is higher than the market price stops producing.

It is, however, less attractive for companies in capital-intensive business sectors to stop producing. A considerable portion of the costs, such as write-offs, carries on even if the company stops. The 'unavoidable' costs are thereby no longer relevant. As long as the market price is higher than the avoidable costs, it is more attractive for a company in a capital intensive business sector to continue doing business than to call a halt. If we look at the steel industry or the paper industry we can see that when times are hard a large number of the companies record losses but that none of them calls it a day. The market price may be below the level of total costs but it is still higher than the avoidable costs.

As a result the price can drop considerably in a capital-intensive sector. To determine where the price might end up we construct the *supply curve* of the business sector (see Figure 5.3). On the basis of the avoidable costs and the capacities of the market players we can sketch the supply curve (because that is what a supply curve is: it shows how much volume the suppliers are willing to produce for what price).

The 'marginal' player's avoidable costs determine the market price (player D in the figure). After all, if the price

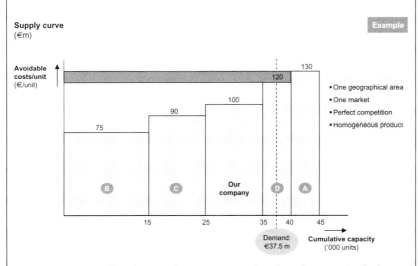

Figure 5.3 Example of a supply curve: price level set by marginal player (D) allows our company to survive and squeezes A out of the market

falls below player D's avoidable costs, then player D will withdraw from the market. As a result demand outstrips supply and prices rise again. The reverse is also true. When the price rises to the avoidable costs level of player E, they will enter the market again. The result of this is overcapacity and downward pressure on prices.

This instrument gives us a good insight into the consequences for the market price of our own behaviour and that of our competitors. What happens to the market price when a competitor increases capacity or improves their cost position?

Take the example of a large-scale household waste collector. This company is paid to collect rubbish and has the waste burned in incinerators by third parties. The company is considering whether to invest in its own incinerator, which can process waste for less than the existing rates. One of the key questions here is whether increasing incinerating capacity will cause a fall in market prices.

This question is answered by means of a supply curve. Waste incineration is a capital-intensive business and the avoidable costs (for avoidable read: variable) are low. For incinerators that generate energy from the heat produced, the avoidable costs are actually negative. Carrying on is then cheaper than stopping because income from the electricity generated is higher than the avoidable costs.

The supply curve for incineration capacity (see Figure 5.4) shows that the gap between the market price and the

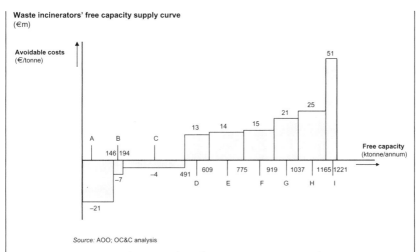

Source: AOO; OC&C analysis

Figure 5.4 Supply curve for electricity generation from waste

avoidable costs is considerable. If the incineration price is €100 the avoidable costs vary between €51 for the 'most expensive' and as little as –€21 for the 'cheapest' incinerator. The risks are thus high. Where there is fierce price competition the price could decline sharply. Whether or not that happens depends on the relationship between supply and demand. Strong price competition only occurs in the case of considerable overcapacity. In order to gain better insight into this relationship, the company also plots the development of supply and demand. Projections of waste volume from local authorities, market players and business organisations, estimations of all ongoing construction projects and the effects of the company's own plan show that the company would definitely cause overcapacity with its plan. The upshot is that the investment of hundreds of millions of pounds is called off.

It is usually no surprise to most team members that profitability can be calculated as the difference between the earnings, which have already been worked out, and the modelled costs. However trivial it is, though, the calculation of profitability nearly always provides valuable, often new or even startling insights. Information that the financial controller has been producing for years is suddenly revealed as being open to other interpretations. Not all products, client segments or channels appear equally attractive. The strict definition of the relevant costs and the correct application of the cost drivers shake up the whole profitability landscape. And if that doesn't throw up ideas for strategic changes in direction, we don't know what will.

Step 1D   Design analyses for the questions – put operational performance under the magnifying glass

Porter says, correctly, that operational effectiveness (on its own) is not a strategy. However, operational qualities must be included in the strategy.

Economies of scale: deceptive myth or attractive reality?

Economies of scale are often cited as important motives for mergers and takeovers. 'With a larger scale we can work with a lower cost structure', or 'If we are larger we can serve more customers'. In practice, however, many of these advantages turn out to be a disappointment. What is more, the effect is sometimes quite the opposite: greater complexity only increases costs, also in relative terms. Let us take an example: a regionally active cleaning firm that takes over a competitor from another part of the country. The advantage of being active throughout the country ('serving clients on a national scale') is limited; the major part of the market buys 'locally' and will continue to do so. Commercial economies of scale are thus small.

Are economies of scale really only a myth or can a larger scale possibly create value? If it can, in which situations is this the case? A sound understanding of economics is a basic requirement here. Try to find out what the most important cost drivers are and analyse whether they depend on scale. In the example of the cleaning firm, the level of management that travels around and oversees the smaller projects is an important source of costs. A driver of these costs is the distance between the various projects that need to be overseen. In order to reduce these costs, as many projects as possible must be concentrated into one particular area. We can achieve economies of scale by acquiring a competitor in the same region.

In many cases operational efficiency can even be of fundamental importance for being able to carry out the chosen plan. For this reason many work plans will include questions, and thus analyses, regarding operational matters. There are a number of possible types of analysis, or combinations thereof.

One analysis is to compare cost prices, preferably for each step in the production process. Make comparisons.

Compare with the past

If no decline can be seen in the cost price – adjusted for inflation – then there is stagnation. Most sectors of industry achieve annual increases in productivity of 3 to 8%, likewise in the service industry changes in working practices can lead to annual reductions in costs.

Compare with potential suppliers

Someone who continues to do something when others can do it more cheaply must have very special reasons for their behaviour. Compare the costs of the various stages of production with the rates of specialised market players.

Where possible, compare with competitors

This comparison is not the easiest to make, but by making effective use of what you know about the competitor's production techniques (ask the machinery supplier, interview your own production experts), what you know about staff numbers (look at the annual report, casually ask the competitor's switchboard operator), and volume (annual report, industry statistics) you can achieve a lot. Don't waste time poring over lots of details but try instead to discover a number of structural factors that can cause costs to vary.

Another analysis concentrates on the characteristics of the manufacturing process. If cost price comparisons with the past, comparisons with suppliers or with competitors are not feasible, we can still get an idea of our place in the operational universe by finding out whether our procedures reflect current views. Although this does not provide any proof regarding our operational performance, as circumstantial evidence it can give us valuable pointers. Let us look at two aspects of this:

- *Compare the technology and techniques used with those of the competitor.* Suppliers of production machinery have a definite interest in saying what the competitor has at their disposal.

- *Compare a number of important performance indicators with current standards.* How many breakdowns do we have to endure, what is the trend concerning the number of faults, how do we score on levels of sick leave, what stock levels do we have, what is our level of debt as a percentage of turnover, etc.?

Step 2   Allocate the tasks

Somebody then has to be made responsible for the analyses. There are at least two ways of dividing up the tasks, of which the first method is usually the one preferred.

Question orientated

If each question is relatively complex and the questions relate to very different fields, it makes sense for each team member to be given the task of answering a complete subsidiary question. Each team member then deals with the analyses linked to the question. This can lead to some inefficiency though, such as when two team members need to interview the same person.

Task orientated

If the questions are less complex it is possible to make a task-orientated division of the work. One team member constructs all the models or interviews a particular expert about topics that relate to various different subsidiary questions. The team manager must ensure that the questions can eventually be answered. After all, the analyses are not an end in themselves, but simply a means of answering a question.

Step 3   Set deadlines

We must set a deadline for each analysis. When should this analysis be finished, considering the time available? How much time do we reasonably need to complete it and which analyses must be done next?

The first version of the work plan does not usually fit within the 11 weeks still remaining. There are of course always arguments in favour of having more time: the diaries of people we want to interview are full, the cost controller who has the data needed is on holiday, constructing a cash flow model takes a lot of time, we don't exactly know our competitor's prices, and so on. But this is not acceptable. The time stipulated, whether the recommended three months or some other period, must not be exceeded before the event. Allocate more capacity or simplify tasks in order to finish on time.

Keep the deadlines simple and watch out for the bureaucrat. As soon as a work plan is made official and company-wide project planning systems have been introduced, the bureaucratic mill begins to grind. Before long someone from a project secretariat phones us to say they want to have a standardised progress report. Next, interdependencies of the various activities have to be set out, the interdependencies with other projects within the company defined and the project taken up into the company-wide milestone analysis. All sorts of graphs with coloured bars and arrows start to stream out of the printer. It doesn't take long before team members are spending half their time on reports and communication. This is unnecessary and a waste of our time. Avoid the official project bureaucrats in the organisation. Do not allow them to include the strategy project in their system and run away quickly with the work plan tucked safely under your arm whenever a bureaucrat heaves into view:

- If the work plan is a good one, its complexity is limited. The project's progress is easy to follow, even without coloured bars and arrows.

- The work plan has a dynamic character. As soon as a hypothesis is shown to be false or new facts appear, the work plan is adjusted, sometimes after just a week. This cannot be achieved within a company's planning package.

- The interdependencies of other projects in the organisation are usually of little relevance. The running time of the strategy project is usually very limited compared with the other projects. What could happen in other projects within three months that would influence the course of the whole company and that the strategy team would not automatically hear about anyway?

6

Allware: the first two weeks

AND THERE SITS JENNY. SHE HASN'T MET HER NEW colleagues yet, she hasn't been given an e-mail account yet, she doesn't even know where her office is and she is already facing the most difficult task of her career. She must find a strategic answer to Allware's problems, a company that she only knows from her job interview. Where should she begin? Who should she involve? What data should she collect?

Opinions and ideas in plenty

Under the circumstances it seems a good idea to Jenny not to start collecting data and making calculations any old how, but to talk first to a significant number of Allware managers. After all, they know the company (and its problems). They are bound to put her on the right track. At the same time it is a good opportunity to introduce herself, to get to know her colleagues and to see which people might play a role in her project team. She gets Schmidt's secretary to organise lots of interviews and luckily, with pressure from the CEO behind it, room in the interviewees' agendas is freed up quickly. Before she knows it her diary is full of appointments.

The interviews are instructive but also very confusing. Everyone seems to think something different is important and to believe in different solutions:

- 'We must carry out a strategic readjustment. Where do we want to go with this company?'

- 'We must alter the company's culture; it must no longer be acceptable for our local managers not to stick to their budgets.'

- 'We operate in mature markets and must therefore reduce our costs in order to maintain our profits. What more can we do to achieve this?'

- 'We carried out a reorganisation two years ago and gave the various countries much more autonomy. That has obviously had a negative effect. We must think up a new organisational structure that does work.'

- 'What acquisitions can we carry out to compensate for our falling turnover?'

- 'We have to make sure that we stay within budget in the next half year, so we must quickly take measures that give results.'

- 'How can we penetrate new growth markets?'

- 'We must get better at keeping abreast of developments: e-business, own brand production in China, introducing key account management, new ERP systems.'

It certainly won't be possible to answer each of these questions and follow up each of these suggestions in three months. Jenny must first of all better understand where the core of the problem lies and which company divisions and ways of improvement she must concentrate on. She decides that to do this she must carry out some analyses.

Getting to the core of the problem

Together with the group controller Jenny establishes a few quick financial comparisons. She first looks at the past; what has actually happened? It appears (see Figure 6.1) that in fact turnover has been falling for years but that the business units have always succeeded in maintaining profit by reducing costs year on year. This only seems to have failed in the last few years, with the result that operational profit has suddenly declined sharply to its current low level.

Thus it appears to be a turnover problem, but should the solution be sought in further efforts to cut costs or can the turnover problem itself be solved? A comparison with the

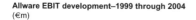

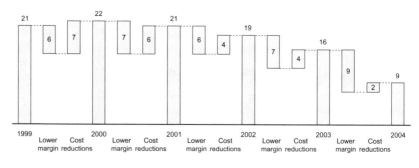

Source: Allware corporate accounts

Figure 6.1 In recent years it has no longer been possible to compensate sales decline by cost reductions

development of market volumes – which Jenny quickly got hold of from the marketing research department – makes it clear that the turnover problem is in any case not directly a market problem. Each of Allware's markets is very mature but there is no question of a decline, except in the offshore market which was under considerable pressure around the turn of the century. However, it is precisely this market that has been enjoying a revival over the last two years – the years in which Allware has been hit hardest – under the influence of high oil prices.

A further comparison with the (scarce) publicly available financial information from competitors shows that Allware actually has a very low level of costs. Further cost reductions will thus not be easy and could be very damaging.

Jenny concludes that the problem is clearly one of a steady loss of market share. That is the problem to which Allware (i.e. Jenny) must find a solution.

Limit the problem further

Although Jenny now has a much better idea of what she needs to concentrate on, she is still worried about how she is to accomplish her mission in three months. Allware is active in all sorts of product groups and in many countries. Does she have to study every one of these markets and find a solution for each of them? Can she perhaps just focus on the largest markets or concentrate on those client segments where the problems are most damaging?

She puts the problem to the group controller, who is quick to reassure her. Allware isn't doing badly everywhere. In the OEM market (which uses Allware's products in their own products) and the pipeline market things are actually going very well, and in shipping the problems are manageable, with the exception of the loss of key customer Pantagruel. The problems seem to be fairly well concentrated as to product segment and geography. To be precise, they are in offshore oil production (UK, the Netherlands and Norway), in the heating sector (Germany and France) and in (petro)chemicals (Western Europe). These three markets together account for 80% of the fall in turnover and, as can be deduced from the profit and loss accounts of the countries in question, for virtually all the decline in profit.

Jenny now has the feeling that she has reduced the problem to bite-sized portions. Over the next three months she will focus on winning market share in the offshore industry, the heating sector and in petrochemicals.

However, the group controller is uneasy. Isn't Jenny being too quick to exclude all sorts of areas of research? Will the company's management accept this from someone who has only been there a few days? How are the managers in, for example, Germany and the offshore industry going to react when the problem is immediately laid at the door of their PMCs, before the whole company has been gone through with a fine-tooth comb? Jenny decides that it is time to discuss her ideas with Schmidt.

A useful talk

'Good that you are here, Jenny,' says Schmidt. 'To be honest, I was on the point of organising a talk with you myself as I'm a bit concerned about how you are getting to grips with things. I had actually expected you to organise a couple of good brain-storming sessions with the country managers, but I hear that so far you have only interviewed them. I haven't seen any big requests for data being sent to the country organisations, and there haven't been any managers coming to me to complain that you want to include their very busy people in your project team. When are you going to start? At this rate we aren't going to make it in three months.'

Despite the awkward start, it turns out to be a good discussion. As Jenny explains to Schmidt what she has done, what she has discovered and how she has broken the problem down into manageable portions, the CEO becomes steadily more enthusiastic.

'Let's move things forward a bit faster,' he says. 'I'll invite the relevant managers to a first meeting where you can present your analyses and we can develop hypotheses together. Then we'll have something to work towards and everybody will be in the know straight away.'

Hypotheses for solving the problem

'Gentlemen,' says Schmidt at the start of the meeting, 'You, Jenny and I are going to get this company back on track. Together we are going to stabilise Allware's turnover and then expand in precisely those segments in which we have been under pressure in the last few years. And we are going to start today. Let us think about why we have lost market share and what we can do about it. And I don't want to hear the words cost reductions today. Over to you, Jenny.'

Jenny, who has of course prepared well for this meeting, leads the managers through her observations and findings. Each manager then says what they think has happened in their market. It is thus revealed that Allware customers in the heating market (a broad assortment of wholesalers who deliver to firms that install heating systems via a network of local outlets) are continually increasing the number of own brands and have extended their product range with products from Allware's competitors.

There is demand in the offshore market for gaskets and appendages but for prices at which it is difficult for Allware to supply them. In petrochemicals, Allware's largest and most international sector, it seems that long-lasting relationships are created between clients and suppliers, but Allware is often

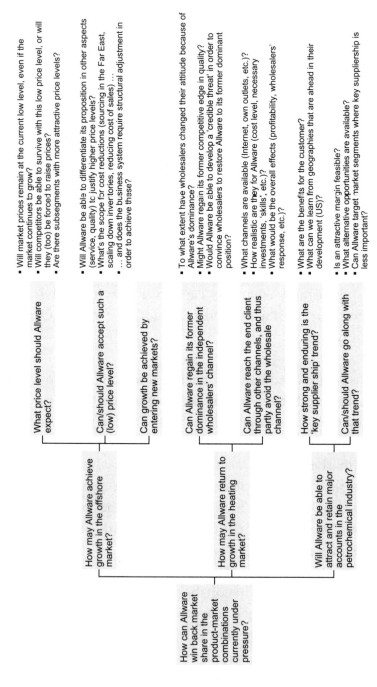

Figure 6.2 Jenny's issue tree

beaten to the worm by an earlier bird, so that relationships are lost for long periods.

At the end of the discussion Jenny puts the results together in an issue tree (see Figure 6.2). This, everyone agrees, should be the foundation of the road to strategic renewal.

Down to work – with focus

Armed with her issue tree and the cooperation of the most important managers, Jenny can now really get down to work. She translates the issue tree into a work plan and a precise request for data and puts together a balanced team of intelligent, analytically minded colleagues from the organisations of the countries concerned, with the addition of the group controller. From now on this project team will report on progress every two weeks to the steering committee of the CEO and the three country managers who are most involved.

Part II – The analysis phase

Introduction

IN THE PREVIOUS PHASE WE FORMULATED THE MOST important analyses but we didn't bother ourselves with how we were going to carry them out. We tried not to think about it because, after all, wasn't there an analysis phase later on? We'd see about it then. But now the analysis phase has begun. This is the point where we are forced to grasp the nettle.

The term analysis phase actually gives the wrong impression. It suggests that analysis is the goal of this phase. In many strategy processes this does appear to be the case. Commercial facts and figures are sliced up into all sorts of tables, histograms and graphs showing market share per region, average prices per product, turnover per month, this per that and x per y, and so on. This produces piles of paper and the information overload just confuses people. At the end of such a presentation rich in tables and graphs, the audience, crushed beneath an avalanche of statistics, cries out in desperation: 'We must develop a vision.' It is a cry for help but even a super-hero may find that all these analyses do not offer much assistance.

The goal of the analysis phase (see Figure II.1) is not to carry out analyses but to answer questions. It would be great if we could answer the questions with sufficient certainty without any analyses, but unfortunately that is not usually possible. Analyses are a necessary evil that demands time and effort. Analyses whose results cannot be used to answer a question are thus a waste of time. Some results are not useful but – you hear someone plead – it's just nice to know them. Someone who wants to develop a strategy in three months, however, can certainly think of nicer things to do than fritter away their time.

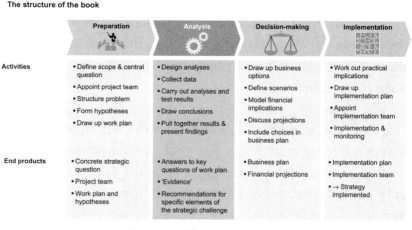

Figure II.1   Phase 2: analysing

In answering the questions, by thinking of analyses and carrying them out, we must choose a sensible level of ambition. The advice here is that these analyses should be factual but not necessarily watertight.

Factual . . .

Opinions are not enough, whether they are the opinions of the board of directors or of the customers. If we want to know whether or not we should merge with a competitor it is not enough to ask: 'Do you think that we ought to merge?' Of course we consult members of the board and customers but mainly to obtain facts.

. . . but not necessarily watertight

In a strategy process we do not look for final proof. Every bit of hard evidence is welcome but it is not available for every question. We should rather try to make something acceptable. In this respect a strategy project resembles a game of chess (make a move according to what your best chance seems to be while the clock is ticking) rather than a trial (only convict if there is no reasonable doubt) or mathematics (only watertight evidence is really evidence).

If customers in neighbouring countries find prices in the supermarket more important than product range or service (and thereby lay the foundations for strong growth in discount stores), they probably behave in the same way in this country, but this is not hard evidence.

At the end of these three weeks we expect to have *probable* answers to the questions from the question tree. We also want to know what conclusion this leads to and what it all means for our company's possible strategy.

7

Days 11 and 12 – We develop the analyses further

What is the goal for these days?

During the preparation phase the team roughly defined the analyses. We are going to look at possible takeover candidates, cross-selling possibilities, etc. Someone is then made responsible for each analysis. So far the team has always operated together but now we divide the work among the team members. Each member gets to work on their own analyses. The first step for everyone is to work out their analyses very concretely – to make them operational. What is today's goal? What are the steps?

Step 1   Break up the problem logically

Many complex ideas appear on closer inspection to be made up of a number of simpler ideas. If you divide the problem into pieces each of the pieces turns out to be easier to handle. We can define different segments, archetypes, categories, axes and so on. This is one of the most important problem-solving techniques: do not just throw everything onto a heap, but chop it up cleverly. The question is: How do we do it cleverly?

Pitfall: a segmentation too far

The business is not a uniform one. For this reason we divide the volume up into segments, each with their own separate characteristics and their own business logic. But if you split volume up too much you can end up with an unmanageably large number of very similar segments. One culprit is the 'multiplication effect'. As soon as we discover, for example, that the domestic market behaves differently from the export market, we are tempted to cut each of the segments that we have already defined into a domestic part and an export part. If we spot a difference between private and business volume – snip – everything is cut into two again. A difference between large and small orders and – snip – before you know it, you have multiplied the number of segments by eight. Maybe the difference between domestic volume and exports is only of significance for business volume, and maybe the difference between private and business customers is only important for small orders, where the volume is too small to be worth considering.

Keep a critical eye on the number of segments. Only include segments where enough volume is involved. Do not automatically split each segment when a distinguishing characteristic is added; only split those segments for which the distinguishing characteristic is relevant.

Avoid overlaps . . .

Anyone who identifies a sales channel labelled 'hotel and catering' and one labelled 'cafés' is asking for confusion, even if it will be clear to many people that in this case hotel and catering does not include cafés. It is more serious if we list, in a time and motion questionnaire, activities such as preparation, sales activities, service activities, consultation and troubleshooting. What should somebody fill in if they are involved in consultation connected with sales activities, for example when preparing an offer? No usable facts will be gleaned from such a questionnaire.

. . . but be complete

Make sure that a list is complete, if necessary by adding the category 'other'. A complete list ensures, for example, that all the turnover figures from the different categories add up to the total turnover.

Don't sift too finely . . .

A segmentation into submarkets or market segments is aimed exclusively at separating various strategic battlegrounds (which we can call the 'games') from each other. If this is not necessary, leave out the segmentation. Segmentation certainly does not come without costs; as soon as a segment is identified we always become curious about turnover and profitability in that segment, about customer behaviour, the competition and so on. Finding all that out requires a lot of work. Therefore, we must try to keep ourselves in check to some extent during this segmentation process. Define a separate segment if 'the game' really is different from that in other segments. Segments can differ in all sorts of areas and it is usually necessary to find differences in more than one area in order to define a new segment:

- *The products are very different,* for example in functionality and price. Our strategy team will thus tend to put SUVs into a different segment from compact cars.

- *The method of production or the distribution shows differences.* Is production capacity completely separated or interchangeable? Do the sales channels differ a lot, with consequences for purchasing behaviour or economics? Think of beer that is sold in supermarkets versus beer served in bars and restaurants.

- *The customers differ from one another.* Think of professional buyers versus private customers or – for a rail company – think of car owners versus people who depend on the train.

. . . but don't use too large a mesh either

Every Dutch person travels on average 10% of the total number of kilometres from home to work by train. But the person who takes the train to work once every two weeks hardly exists. Working with averages – mixing apples and pears – often throws up unusable information. Recognise when you need to split up groups.

Step 2   Set priorities

As we are not sure whether we will manage to finish everything, we start with the most important sections or segments, with no more depth or precision than is strictly necessary. Then, if we discover later that we have time left, or if it appears on closer inspection that more detail is really essential, we can always add sections or segments, delve deeper or achieve greater precision. But first we must deal with the big chunks and get a rough picture.

The 80/20 rule

Anyone who has worked for many years as a strategy consultant has inevitably spent a lot of time with other consultants. Leaving aside whether this was a pleasant or an unpleasant experience, the fact is that consultancy jargon stays with you. There are some concepts that we can no longer stand hearing, and in this book you won't come across ideas such as 'win–win situation', 'thinking out of the box', 'garbage in/garbage out', 'retail is detail'.

However, one concept cannot be left out because, however well worn it is, it still contains a powerful kernel of truth. This is the 80/20 rule.

The 80/20 rule indicates an uneven division, for example if 80% of turnover is earned from just 20% of the (largest) clients, or if 80% of the gross margin is generated from just 20% of the (best) products. This is of course not literally true. It may very well be that 60% of turnover comes from 30% of clients, or 95% from 15% of clients (it doesn't have to add up to 100%). But the basic idea of the 80/20 rule is often spot on and its implicit advice is sensible: look first at the big pieces of your puzzle and, when you have done that, you will already have achieved a lot. Then ask yourself whether you need to look at the rest. In short, set sensible priorities in your work.

Focus

Once the segments have been defined, the size of the task becomes clear. Do we need analyses for all these segments? We hope not. Ask yourself the following questions:

- Do all the segments contribute enough in terms of turnover and their (potential) contribution? If not, leave the small fry for later.

- Are interim conclusions for one segment likely to be the same as those for another segment? If so, put the segments together (see above).

DAYS 11 AND 12 / **101**

- Is one segment much easier to analyse than the other? If so, do the easy analyses first. Remember that easy analyses do not necessarily provide less insight than difficult analyses.

Precision

Use analyses above all to make an answer *acceptable*, rather than to *prove* an answer with mathematical certainty. The latter is in any case not possible and even to attempt it will put our three-month timetable in danger.

Depth

If you analyse a market player who is in the business of door furniture, you will understand that hinges are something very different from door handles. But wouldn't 90% of the conclusions for hinges also be valid for door handles? In that case we will first examine the whole.

Step 3   Choose a type of analysis

We have now decided what we are going to analyse (day 5), what kind of segmentation is appropriate and what our priorities are. However, one important question has not yet been addressed: How? How are we going to do these analyses? How can we ensure that by putting together facts and logic we can eventually answer the subsidiary questions? In short, what does the analysis really look like? We will 'look' at the cross-selling possibilities, but what do we mean by look? It must mean more than just having a look.

Do not look for support from standardised frameworks. Many academics, but also members of staff responsible for strategy, swear, for example, by the well-known SWOT analysis. However, leading strategy companies use this framework at most to come up with ideas and not to find serious answers to relevant questions. Because our questions are not standardised, the analysis isn't either. We need to find a logic that fits the questions. Here we can choose between several options.

A comparison versus a driver analysis

The most popular technique for making forecasts is extrapolation, or projecting the line on into the future. This is almost bound to go wrong. Better options are the driver analysis and the comparison with other markets or market players (see Figure 7.1):

- In a driver analysis we first determine what *drives* a particular quantity that we want to predict, such as market size. First of all we work out in theory what could have an influence on market size, before testing these assumptions on the basis of historical data. Some typical drivers for market size are factors such as population size, gross domestic product, per capita purchasing power, construction volume or total office floor space. It usually boils down to between two and five real drivers, for which there are reasonable forecasts. The historical data also show how much influence the driver has on market develop-

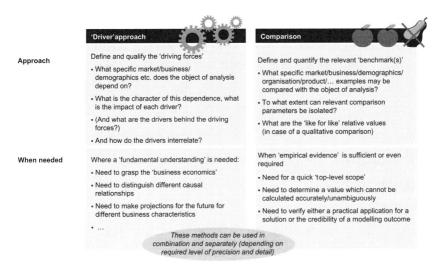

Figure 7.1 Two important analytical approaches

ment. Does the driver have a major or only a minor effect? Once we know what the drivers of market size are, how they develop and to what extent this influences market size, we have a growth indicator.

- In a comparison analysis we begin by looking for countries, situations or market players, which are in principle comparable with the country, the situation or the market player for which we wish to make a forecast. Next we compare the relevant quantities as a basis for a forecast. Let us say that the comparison indicates that television advertising rates in more developed advertising markets are higher than those in our own country. We must then estimate whether the rates here are likely to rise over time. It is more effective to combine the comparison with a sound understanding of the drivers. If the advertising rates are linked to the amount of broadcasting time available for commercials (because of legislation, for instance) we must include these details in our comparison. Then we do not simply compare countries, we display the countries on a graph with the available broadcasting time on one axis and the advertising rates on the other.

Benchmarking: comparing apples with apples

How do you answer questions such as: 'Can costs be reduced further?' or: 'Can turnover per salesperson be increased?' One of the quickest and most frequently used methods for this is benchmarking. If competitor X has considerably lower unit costs than we have, it means that we can perhaps reduce our costs. If we sell 40% more per salesperson in country Y than in country Z, then we should be able to improve our commercial efficiency significantly in the latter country. Benchmarking doesn't actually provide a direct answer to the question of *how* we should improve, but it does give an indication of how much potential there is.

The idea behind benchmarking is simple. In order to benchmark cost positions for example, you define a 'product unit' and compare the costs incurred by different players or company divisions in producing that unit. In practice, however, benchmarking is not always so simple. It often turns out to be difficult to compare apples with apples. Figures are often only available at a high level of aggregation, so that you are more likely to be comparing baskets of mixed fruit (with different assortments). It is also not always clear whether the same definitions are being used. What one person calls an apple, another thinks is more of a pear.

Even if you don't have these problems, comparisons are not as self-evident as they might seem. Each apple is different. Cost benchmarking in the airline industry can be used to illustrate this point and, at the same time, show how you can correct for the differences in types of apple.

Defining the unit (the apple) in the airline industry seems simple. You can take costs per passenger per flight or costs per passenger per kilometre. However, if you compare a long-haul flight with a short flight, you discover that the two units are not equal. Obviously the costs per passenger per flight for the long-haul flight will be higher than for the short flight as the aircraft is in the air longer, uses more fuel and cannot make any other flights during this time (which means higher capital costs and labour costs). But the costs per passenger per kilometre also fail to give an honest picture. After all, both aircraft use up the same amount of time in taxiing, letting passengers embark, clocking staff in and out and cleaning. Moreover, a significant proportion of the fuel is used for taking off, which means that a short flight uses more fuel per kilometre. In other words, one unit 'favours' the short flight, while the other unit 'favours' the long journey. Thus, if you compare airlines that differ greatly in (average) flight distance, you cannot use either unit directly for benchmarking.

There is a solution, however. You can adjust the costs for flight distance! To do this you establish for each flight which elements are fixed and which are dependent on the distance covered during the flight (see Figure 7.2). This allows you to determine per cost element (fuel, crew, capital costs, cleaning, etc.) in what way these elements are dependent on flight distance (see Figure 7.3 for some examples). It then becomes clear that the cost of the crew is linearly dependent on the flight distance, but with a large fixed component per flight (due to all the fixed, time-consuming activities before take-off and after landing). Catering costs increase in stages, as on a short flight only a cup of coffee is served, on slightly longer journeys a sandwich is added and on longer flights still there might be a second cup of coffee. By adding up all the cost elements again we can calculate the total costs per unit as a function of the flight distance.

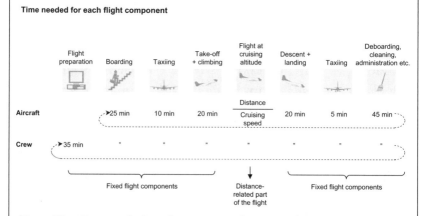

Figure 7.2 Crew and aircraft costs in relation to distance covered are determined by the mix of 'fixed' and 'variable' flight components

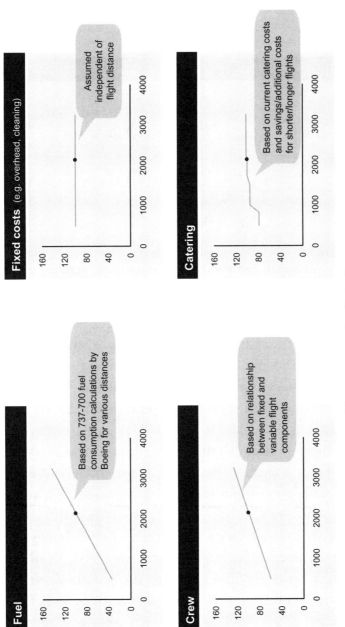

Figure 7.3 Model corrections for flight distance per cost centre

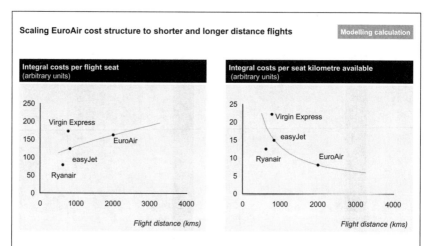

Figure 7.4 When corrected for differences in average flight distance, EuroAir overall cost position can be compared with low cost airlines

This is done in Figure 7.4 for the (fictitious) airline EuroAir. The average flight distance for this airline is more than 2000 km. A direct comparison with low cost competitors such as easyJet and Virgin Express is not possible, as these companies have average flight distances of less than 1000 km. By calculating EuroAir's costs to take account of these shorter distances, benchmarking is made possible. EuroAir appears to be about as cost efficient as easyJet but there is clear room for improvement in comparison with Ryanair. By also comparing these 'unit costs corrected for flight distance' with each other for each cost element (crew, overheads, airport costs, etc.) it is possible to pinpoint more accurately where the potential for improvement can be found. You can also work out what measures are necessary (such as a different collective agreement for the crew or using cheaper, secondary airports) in order to overtake Ryanair.

A complete data analysis versus a sample or examples

The PC has more or less eliminated the sample from our vocabulary as its enormous data-processing capacity allows us to include 'everything'. Samples are, however, still worth considering. For a large amount of data we often need to use a more complex database application, whereas a sample can often be handled with a simple spreadsheet. Instead of analysing all customers and all products, an example or a sample often does the job. Remember that watertight proof is not required of a team that has to define a complete strategy in three months. It is enough to have plausible conclusions. Compare these two situations:

- In a situation where, for example, a small number of very large clients account for the bulk of turnover, it doesn't make much sense to lump all turnover together. After all, why work with statistical data if you can also look very specifically at a number of large clients that really exist? In this case a sample could even be dangerous; the sample that includes the large client (small probability) gives a very different result from a sample without the client (large probability), and neither is representative. Here it is preferable to work with a limited number of examples of large clients, possibly with the addition of a sample from the rest.

- In a situation where there are a large number of more or less comparable clients, a sample is a good idea. Representative results can then be reached without too much effort and without having to wrestle with the whole mass of data.

Bottom-up versus top-down

A *bottom-up* analysis constructs a particular concept or figure out of the constituent parts. An example of a bottom-up analysis is a cost calculation in which the total costs are calculated by determining the different expenses one after another then adding them up. A bottom-up calculation often provides a detailed concept. It gives insight into how and why you can achieve something.

A *top-down* analysis starts out from the total picture to construct a concept. An example of a top-down calculation is a comparison of the total costs of different competitors. How, where and why the costs differ is not always made clear in detail, but we can see that one refinery has higher costs per barrel than the other one. Although this is more of a black box approach, it is a way of estimating potential, determining orders of magnitude or setting goals. It gives insight into *whether* you can achieve something but it usually doesn't say *how*.

Say the question tree contains the question: 'Can working capital be reduced?' Some bottom-up analyses that answer this question are: (1) split total working capital into categories, such as debtors, creditors, etc.; (2) carry out a number of analyses for each category. For the debtors category this could be done as follows:

- Arrange the list of debtors by the 'age' of the debt (histogram).

- Analyse 'prompting' behaviour (reminders, telephone calls and other measures to ensure payment) in relation to how long the payment has been outstanding, etc.

With such a bottom-up approach we look at whether things can be done better in each separate area. A top-down way of answering this question would be to compare the amount of debt owed to us, as a percentage of turnover, with leading competitors. This top-down analysis offers no insight into *how* the level of debt can be reduced but it can show *whether* there is a chance of achieving this. The most convincing results are achieved through a combination of top-down and bottom-up.

Qualitative versus quantitative analysis

Many companies, when deciding on strategy, get bogged down in qualitative arguments when faced with a choice that is essentially based on vision (or feeling). It is best if the qualitative arguments are translated into financial prognoses at the end of the strategy-forming process, though these prognoses are based more on aims (*I want*) than on well-founded expectations (*I can*). In our experience, however, sense and nonsense can best be kept apart by using figures.

Make the analyses as factual as possible, preferably with quantitative facts. Numbers help to distinguish large from small, important from unimportant and favourable from unfavourable. Not everything is quantifiable but those who try to quantify get further than those who work in a purely qualitative way. Don't trust pluses and minuses to indicate the size or attractiveness of a market. One plus is not the same as another. Anyone who isn't exactly sure is better off using a bandwidth.

Step 4 Determine a (temporary) format for the end product

Define an end product during the analyses. With a well-formulated analysis you can imagine what the result, the *end product*, will look like. Is the end product a figure, a table, a graph, a list or an organisation chart? The team members are more focused in their work if they rough out the table or graph even before the analysis has been started, as a kind of dummy run. The team manager assesses these drafts and uses them to help in supervising progress.

Example: the significance of figures

Suppose a travel company is considering scrapping traditional ticket sales in order to switch completely to booking via the Internet, using electronic security. The questions are whether the customer will accept this and how much money it will save.

A purely qualitative method would be one based on comparison. Airline ABC and holiday home letting company FGH have already taken this step. In addition, market research organisation XYZ claims studies have shown that customers consider the Internet to be almost as important a sales outlet as the physical travel agent.

Finally, information from interviews shows that companies can save a lot of money by making such a switch. This gives some confidence in the first instance. If others do it, why shouldn't we? But why hasn't everybody in the market taken this step? Is the time perhaps still not ripe?

A semi-quantitative method shows, for example, what proportion of the population, or what proportion of current travellers, has Internet access and how quickly this is growing. To accompany this you could consider the figures for the volume and growth of total consumer sales via the Internet. To finish off you can calculate the costs that can be saved on the balance sheet. This provides more of an insight into the value of certain determining quantities, but it does not yet indicate what the connections are between these quantities. Is the switch to online sales a good idea at this time? After all, there are still customers without Internet access. Can we risk losing them?

A fully quantified analysis completes the above picture by adding information on what proportion of the current clientele can be lost before the cost advantage is matched by loss of margin. What is the relationship between this group and the group of non-Internet users? What are the costs involved in possibly continuing conventional ticket sales for a time? Would it be reasonable to transfer these costs to the customers themselves by means of a supplement?

A quantified analysis doesn't completely banish the darkness and provide absolute certainty, but it does limit subjectivity and makes it possible to form judgements about the same facts in a much more organised fashion. A final decision still requires estimates and subjective judgements by management, but the area within which these judgements have to be made is limited and better defined. It is not so easy to evaluate whether or not we should transfer to online sales if we only know that ABC is doing it, as in the qualitative analysis. It is also not so easy to make the decision if we know, say, that 81% of our customers have an Internet connection, as shown in the semi-quantitative analysis. Is that enough or too little? Subjectivity is further reduced, and we are thus better able to form judgements, if we know that financial results improve as soon as more than 72% of customers are able to make the switch to buying online. The quantitative analysis offers the most help towards a carefully considered judgement, without any new data being added.

Characteristics of desirable end products | Indicative

When defining envisaged end products	The ultimate end products should ...
• Set unambiguous content and process objectives for specific team members	• Meet agreed requirements (in terms of content, timing, shape, level of detail)
• Make sure envisaged end products are aligned with the work plan logic, to ensure that outcomes provide answers to relevant questions	• Specifically answer questions listed in the work plan, and offer clues for possible consequences and follow-up questions
• Envisaged end products should help team members/ provide clues when doing the analyses	• Be clearly founded on relevant data and analyses (backups!)
• Preferably, leave room for team members' own contribution and creativity	• As much as possible (i.e. not to the utmost!) reflect the understanding and creativity of those responsible for them
• Make sure envisaged end products are realistic in terms of content, timing, shape, level of detail, ...	• Give an accurate and realistic picture, with disclaimers insofar as acceptable and necessary

Figure 7.5 Aim for specific, practical end products as much as possible

Defining an end product is a measure that really boosts productivity (see Figure 7.5). If a person knows which table they are supposed to produce they have less cause to make unproductive digressions and run less risk of losing sight of the goal. Working 'back to front' is well worth it; working with a specific end product in mind is much more effective than doing some work and then seeing which end product it leads to.

8

Days 13 to 17 – We collect data

What is the goal for these days?

After defining the analyses there is another concern, which we have also been able to suppress up to now, and that is the problem of data collection. Where do we find all the facts that we need in order to carry out the analyses?

A possible source of information is of course in the first instance an earlier analysis. How often have you heard someone say: 'We've already investigated that. It must be on the shelf here somewhere.' Sadly this is often disappointing as it turns out that the work was not recorded or there are only a few summarising diagrams, or the analysis was about something just slightly different, it is out of date or not split into the segments that you now believe to be the relevant ones. Don't put too much faith in that shelf.

So the team has to collect a large number of usable facts in a short time. The word 'usable' is of fundamental significance here. We are not looking for the absolute truth, precision is usually not necessary and we don't need to know everything. We must concentrate on the usable facts, the facts that are sufficient to answer the questions.

It is essential to establish first what data we need. Know what you want to know. What is the appropriate time horizon? What time scale do we need for the analyses: three years or 10 years? How detailed do the facts have to be: do we need turnover per month or per year? How precise must the data be: can we use a population figure expressed in millions or do we need to know exactly how many thousand people there are? Be mindful of the explosion effect. Someone makes a complex request for data (such as all the turnover figures per product group, per country and per account) then, just as the data manager is walking out of the room, that person calls after him: 'Oh yes, just to be sure, get the turnover breakdown per month and do it for the last three years after all.' The whole database has just been expanded by a factor of 36.

There is a multitude of ways to find out what we need to know (see Figure 8.1). We will consider a number of methods below, methods that overlap to some extent.

Make internal data available

The facts may not be lying on the shelf but they are there somewhere, possibly in another form. A lot of information is available within the organisation:

Figure 8.1 Be creative when searching for data: the facts are out there in the street!

The client base

This source of information is a valuable basis for all sorts of customer analyses. Make sure that you obtain the data in multidimensional form (i.e. in the form of databases) rather than in all kinds of separate intersections (in the form of tables, for example).

Using separate intersections you can establish, for instance, that we incur relatively high sales costs with a quarter of our customers, and that a quarter of the customers mainly place large orders. But whether this is the same quarter in both cases (probably not entirely) is only made clear in a multi-dimensional database.

The financial system

We obtain the costs from the financial system but, as we mentioned earlier, they probably won't be in the form of standardised reports. Spend time first with the cost controller in order to define costs correctly. In order to perform a good cost analysis, based on cost drivers, take the cost *centres* first, so as to be able to plot the activities. Then, within each individual activity, delve into the cost *types*, in order to model cost behaviour.

Be extremely critical with regard to cost allocations. These are usually unsuitable for your purpose. The only solution is often to get rid of the cost allocation and evaluate it anew.

It is usually not enough to call the cost controller or the marketing manager and explain over the phone what you need in order to obtain the correct data from these sources. It is not easy to formulate a precise and comprehensive request for information yourself and the person at the other end of the line is very likely to misinterpret your complicated tale or forget the details. If you ask, for example, for turnover per segment per region, don't be surprised if you get one list with turnover per segment and another list with turnover per region. Unfortunately it is not possible to work out the turnover from segment X in region Y from these lists. We must thus draw up a clear written request for data:

- *Be clear about what you need the data for*, so that the data provider can think with you. If appropriate bring in facts that you have discovered yourself. Take account of the confidentiality of the project and of the data provider's own interests. They may possibly have their own agenda, which is not in line with the rest of the project organisation.

- *Draft the data format*, preferably in an empty table or on an empty database sheet. This will help to clarify what we are looking for 'per unit of what'. Define the various different elements that make up the data. What do we mean by an 'order'? Name the units in which the figures that you have requested should be expressed (units of currency, numbers, ratios). Don't forget net versus gross, with or without VAT, before or after deduction of sales costs, this year versus last year, etc.

- *Specify the medium* in which you want the information. Do you want to receive the data digitally or on paper? If in digital form, what sorts of data formats can you work with?

- *Discuss a realistic deadline.* Ask to see some data in advance in order to see what the quality is and what a reasonable deadline might be. If the deadline is too far away, consider whether you couldn't also start work with less information (fewer fields of investigation, fewer records). Make clear which figures are essential and which would just be nice to have. You could perhaps offer to help in gathering the data.

Don't forget to thank your data supplier afterwards for all their work. Tell them – as long as the rules of confidentiality allow it – what the result of the analysis was. They might be able to help you check its validity. People who have access to huge quantities of figures must be treasured as friends. They are the lifeblood of the team. Give the data providers feedback, too. The feedback will help them to provide you with (even) better data in future.

Conduct interviews

We cannot find all the data we need on an electronic database. Our customers, sector experts, even our own colleagues are walking sources of information, even if you wouldn't think this when you bump into them by the coffee machine. We are going to use interviews to garner their knowledge.

Interviews are a greatly *overestimated* but at the same time *underused* form of research. Many people seem to think that the purpose of an interview is to ask others for the answers to our subsidiary questions, as in: 'Do you think that our company should make an acquisition?' This is to over-estimate the usefulness of an interview. Most people do not know the answer to this question. How would they know? And why else would the question have been asked of our team? Some individual may well know the answer but how do we know that they know? This type of interview behaviour leads to the interview being underused, that is to say not exploited properly. It produces at best nothing and at worst nonsense.

An interview will not give you an answer to the subsidiary questions. But interviews are extremely useful for finding out facts that are needed to answer the questions. Not all facts come from statistics. You can get a large amount of data from the people in the know: the interview candidates.

Prepare the interview well

In order to get everything possible out of an interview, we must first prepare it well (see Figure 8.2). If you just 'have a chat' you will be disappointed and the interviewee will also be justified in being disappointed. A thorough preparation contains the following steps:

- Get the work plan and think about what data or views you want to glean from the interview. The aim of an interview is generally to collect a fact and to help with a subsidiary

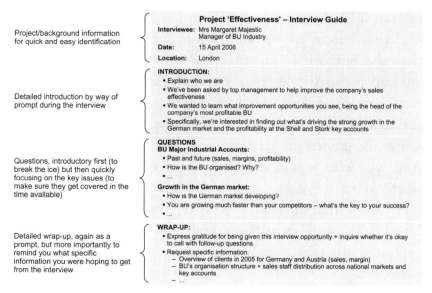

Project/background information
for quick and easy identification

Detailed introduction by way of
prompt during the interview

Questions, introductory first (to
break the ice) but then quickly
focusing on the key issues (to
make sure they get covered in the
time available)

Detailed wrap-up, again as a
prompt, but more importantly to
remind you what specific
information you were hoping to get
from the interview

Project 'Effectiveness' – Interview Guide
Interviewee: Mrs Margaret Majestic
Manager of BU Industry
Date: 15 April 2006
Location: London

INTRODUCTION:
• Explain who we are
• We've been asked by top management to help improve the company's sales effectiveness
• We wanted to learn what improvement opportunities you see, being the head of the company's most profitable BU
• Specifically, we're interested in finding out what's driving the strong growth in the German market and the profitability at the Shell and Stork key accounts

QUESTIONS
BU Major Industrial Accounts:
• Past and future (sales, margins, profitability)
• How is the BU organised? Why?
• ...

Growth in the German market:
• How is the German market developing?
• You are growing much faster than your competitors – what's the key to your success?
• ...

WRAP-UP:
• Express gratitude for being given this interview opportunity + inquire whether it's okay to call with follow-up questions
• Request specific information:
  – Overview of clients in 2005 for Germany and Austria (sales, margin)
  – BU's organisation structure + sales staff distribution across national markets and key accounts
  – ...

Figure 8.2 A structured interview guide is very useful

question from our work plan. If the question is, for example: 'How can we improve our sales procedures?', we must, among other things, analyse what the purchasing cycle of our clients looks like. Who decides what, when and on the basis of what considerations? What this cycle looks like cannot be found anywhere, it can only be made clear through interviews. (On occasion we can also collect hypotheses through interviews. This is not the kind of interview we are referring to here.)

• Decide who we are going to interview. Who can be expected to answer the questions? Would that person be prepared to be interviewed? Do we have the right connections?

• Allow for some give and take. While some people still think it flattering that someone should want to interview them, others are fed up with altruistically answering questions. And those are precisely the interviewees who are most in demand and most valuable! Consider whether we might also have something to offer. Could we promise to give the interview candidate our market analysis?

- Find out about the person to be interviewed. What is their current position and what is their background? It would surely be a shame to find out only after the event that the person in question had worked for a major competitor in the recent past, or that you had both studied at the same faculty.

- Prepare a list of topics, possibly with questions for each topic. What can I talk about and what is confidential for this person? What are this person's interests? What is at stake for them? What have they got to win or lose if they give certain answers? Make sure that the questions are in a logical order. Start with general questions but then come quickly to the point. If it is desirable that the interviewee prepare themselves a bit for the interview as well it could be useful to send them the topics list in advance.

Extract the right information

It goes without saying that we must be on time, introduce ourselves, remain polite and try to make it a pleasant discussion for the interviewee as well. During the interview we must of course also make sure that we obtain the right information. For this we must steer the interview a bit:

- As a rule, go to the interview together with someone else. You often find that you then get more out of the talk.

- Forestall endless digressions. Not only are interviewers sometimes mistaken about the nature of interviews. Interviewees, too, tend to think that their opinion is being sought on all sorts of things. Perhaps they are in favour of that takeover and would like to discuss it in great detail.

- Use the list of topics or the questions as a basis for the talk. Hand out the list or write it clearly on the board for the interviewee. This helps them to stay on message. Many people have the tendency to just 'work their way through the list' first.

- Formulate or visualise a possible answer or structure for an answer. If we want to understand the purchasing cycle it is a good idea to put down on paper a number of possible stages in that process. If the reality is different we will hear it from our interviewee. People find it easier to make changes to an existing concept than to set up something completely new in an hour or so.

- Sum up the discussion and test possible conclusions: 'So, if I have understood you correctly, your past experiences with a supplier are of very little importance for you in the choice of a future supplier?'

- Create the possibility of a follow-up: 'Would it be possible to come back to you at a later stage to test our conclusions further?' Thank the interviewee for their time and useful insights! Afterwards, send them a thank you letter.

Make the results available to the team

Process the interview immediately. This helps you to avoid forgetting relevant details. Provide a clear description of the situation and background of the interviewee. Draw conclusions from the talk. Try already to answer, at least in part, the relevant subsidiary question. Set down the results concisely in an interview report. Structure the report by topic or by conclusion as a chronological account is of no use. If the interviewee made some telling or salient remarks, give direct quotes. In addition, mention logical further steps that emerge from the interview.

Collect data on business sectors and competitors

A lot of data on business sectors can be bought. Don't be scared off by a high price. Good answers to fundamental questions are worth their weight in gold, and we have already scrapped the non-fundamental questions from the list. Don't forget:

- Business sector organisations often work only on behalf of members. Our simple advice is to become a member.

- Independent research organisations often produce a periodic overview of a sector, containing all sorts of statistics (often very usable) and a discussion of the most important trends (useful for inspiring ideas but sometimes just a lot of nonsense). Buy it!

We can also find out quite a lot about specific competitors, while keeping our hands clean:

- Interview their customers, the middlemen and their (logistical) suppliers. Use these parties, many of whom we already have a relationship with, to get to know the competitor better.

- Interview their former employees. Do some of them now work for our own organisation?

- Study the competitor's annual report. This will tell us something about developments in turnover, margins, costs structure, staff levels and the most important strategic initiatives.

Calculate your own data

If particular data are missing we can perhaps calculate them ourselves. We leave surveys of thousands of consumers to specialised organisations, but we can easily manage a lot of data collection ourselves. Here are a few examples.

Carry out consumer research

Consumer research is sometimes necessary but it is time consuming and expensive. You can ask yourself whether detailed consumer research is really essential for a strategic project. Most such research is part of product development or marketing projects.

Organise time and motion surveys

The cost controller apportions the time of sales and service staff to turnover in proportion to their numbers, but how do our people really spend their time? Organise a time and motion survey for the colleagues in question. In most cases you can achieve a lot in a week. On the time and motion questionnaire make a distinction between what a person devotes their time to (which goal, channel, client, product, etc.) and what the person actually does in that time (travelling, visiting a client, preparing documents, etc.).

Visit shops

In order to gain a clear impression of our (consumer goods) competitors' positions we visit shops. How does our competitor arrange their distribution, where is he positioned on the shelves, what kind of range and price level does he have? Of course we do not just walk into a shop unprepared to 'get an impression'. That impression will have vanished by the following day and five weeks later all that we will be able to tell the steering committee will be that 'it all looked very nice'. If we really want to gain something from the shop visits we must set to work in a structured way:

- Consider beforehand what data you require. Prepare a manageable form to fill in so that you don't have to sit in the shop scribbling in notepads balanced on your knee. Make sure that you can just tick the points that you need.

- Take a camera (product concepts, positions on the shelves) and a tape recorder (prices) with you, so as to be able to record information in other ways as well.

- If you wish to, try to talk to the manager of the shop. Prepare the questions and make an appointment. However, most store managers are rather suspicious of this kind of data collection so don't count on too much cooperation. The national category manager of the chain will usually not cooperate at all, even after an introduction from your own sales manager. You are the third manufacturer this week who wants to talk to them about trends in his category.

- If the shop doesn't want to cooperate, which frequently occurs, make sure that you go unnoticed. Take a trolley and buy something. Don't go walking around in a pin-striped suit with a large form clutched to your chest. Make sure that you have an answer to the question: 'What's that you're noting down?' It isn't against the law to visit shops but it is worth being cautious.

Mystery shopping

There is no better way of understanding the behaviour of salespeople, middlemen and service providers than to become a customer yourself and get involved in the business by doing some mystery shopping (see Figure 8.3). Get inside the skin of a customer and investigate in what way your own or, especially, competing products are recommended, what kind of service the competitor provides, what the competitor's offer consists of, and so on.

Findings of shop visits: price differences for A brands | Example

Product	Brand	Volume	Unit	Retailer A	Retailer B	Retailer C	Retailer D	Retailer E
Strawberry jam	Hero	400	grammes	1.55	1.69	1.65	1.69	1.69
Washing-up liquid	Dubro citroen	500	ml	0.94	0.90	0.95	0.99	0.99
Apple sauce	HAK	720	ml	0.63	0.72	0.72	0.72	0.72
Biscuit rusk	Bolletje	13	pieces	0.51	0.53	0.53	0.57	0.57
Mineral water	Spa reine	1500	ml	0.44	0.45	0.45	0.45	0.45
Crisps (unflavoured)	Lay's	200	grammes	0.72	0.75	0.75	0.75	0.75
Chocolate	Verkade	75	grammes	0.69	0.76	0.79	0.79	0.87
Coke (regular)	Coca-Cola	1500	ml	0.92	0.93	0.95	0.95	0.95
Orange juice	Appelsientje	1000	ml	0.82	0.83	0.83	0.87	1.05
Cat food	Whiskas Adult	400	grammes	0.73	0.75	0.79	0.79	0.79
Chewing gum	Sportlife	48	pieces	1.49	1.55	1.55	1.59	1.59
Frankfurters	Unox	200	grammes	0.95	0.97	0.97	1.02	1.02
Coffee (extra-fine ground)	Douwe Egberts	500	grammes	2.29	2.39	2.39	2.39	2.39
Macaroni	Honig	500	grammes	0.48	0.49	0.49	0.49	0.49
Olive oil	Bertolli Classico	500	ml	3.59	3.59	3.79	3.85	3.59
Peanut butter	Calvé	350	grammes	1.18	1.05	1.19	1.05	1.09
Peanuts	Duyvis	250	grammes	0.95	0.99	0.99	1.05	1.05
Minute rice	Lassie	400	grammes	0.78	0.79	0.79	0.82	0.82
Sugar	CSM	1000	grammes	0.83	0.87	0.89	0.89	0.88
Tea	Pickwick	80	grammes	0.75	0.81	0.81	0.81	0.81
Fish fingers	Iglo	300	grammes	1.37	1.37	1.37	1.37	1.37
Total				**22.61**	**23.17**	**23.74**	**23.90**	**23.93**

Source: Store checks; OC&C analysis

Figure 8.3 Mystery shopping can yield valuable insights – example: A-brand prices are roughly the same across Dutch 'service supermarkets'

Here, too, thorough preparation is the key to success. If you want to map out what happens during the sales process, divide the process into stages beforehand and consider which aspects you want to measure for each stage. If the aim is to discover a competitor's commercial conditions, ask for a special offer.

Filling in missing facts ourselves

Then we find that we are still missing a few things. In some cases we have to put together the required insights without being able to use ready-made facts.

Suppose we want to know the relative cost position of our factory and data on the competitor's costs do not appear to be available. We can then construct these data by approximation, as follows:

- Accept that we are not going to find out the *real, up-to-date* cost position of our competitor. We have to make do with the *structural* cost position as it would be if all competitors were equally ingenious and dynamic. We cannot, of course, recreate all sorts of chance factors in the cost position. This approximation of the cost position looks more towards the long term than if we were to take the current costs. Isn't that exactly what we want anyway?

- Bring in those structural variations between the different market players that are expected to have an influence on costs. Consider distances to major suppliers or clients, structural differences in energy prices, differences in processes or technology, variations in wage costs and so on.

- Determine by what percentage each competitor and each structural variation affects which particular expenses. Use your own cost position as a starting point for calculating the competitors' percentages. Where the factor costs differ, the percentages are simply related to the ratio of the factor costs. You need to think a bit more about differences in technology, for example. Estimate, for instance, the capacity of the competitor's production machinery and then estimate how many workers are needed to man the production line. Set these ratios against those in your own organisation in order to calculate the differences in wage costs per unit.

- Next, determine the cost structure for each competitor by relating the percentage differences to the sources of costs in your own cost structure.

- Check the results with experts and discount possible non-structural but well-known and 'stubborn' influences. In this way we have created a defensible cost structure in the business sector, without having any direct cost data.

9

Days 18 to 42 – We carry out the analyses

What is the goal for these days?

After thoughts come deeds. The analyses have been defined, the data collected and now the analyses have to be carried out. There is no generic recipe for performing a 'typical' analysis, so in this chapter we will simply give some guidelines and some advice. What steps can we take?

Step 1 Test the inputs

Even quite substantial analyses are often based on a limited number of essential facts and calculations. Without going into all aspects of the analysis, the team should look at these inputs critically before doing the analysis:

- Look for the unbelievable numbers, which always manage to sneak in. Only when you do the calculation do you discover a figure that indicates that every inhabitant drinks two litres of beer a day (the figure gives total drinks consumption instead of just beer, or a comma has shifted, or maybe the figure is for production and not consumption). Ask yourself whether sensitive figures are logical.

- Make sure that figures have the same basis. Check that the amounts quoted are defined for the same year, that sales tax has already been excluded, check whether it is net or gross, and so on. Is there real growth or are we looking at exchange rate fluctuations?

- Make the connection with the whole. Do the turnover figures per product group really add up to the total turnover or has somebody forgotten to add in the associated services? If you perform the 'totals test' you might drive your data supplier to despair, but despair before the analysis is preferable to despair afterwards.

Step 2   Carry out the analyses as planned

In week three we specified the analyses. There is nothing more to add to that here. Make sure that decisions (working methods, suppositions, use of data) are well documented or later on nobody will understand anything any more.

Step 3   Test the outcomes

Is the outcome of the analysis believable? Every analysis deserves a sanity check. Ask the team a few questions:

- How sensitive are the analyses? What happens if the underlying suppositions are changed by the analyses? How great an influence do external factors have on the analyses?

- Can changes in trends be explained? Costs rose previously by 1% per year. Do we really expect them to fall by 20% over the next three years? It may be possible but without a convincing explanation it is not very acceptable.

- Is the current situation correct? Someone who constructs a business economic model, in which all sorts of inputs lead to a business economic outcome, can easily test the model. Put in the current situation and see whether the current situation comes out. If the current situation itself is not accurate, there is a strong chance that the modelled variants will not be correct.

International data

Those who use data from international databases must watch out. Sometimes monetary data (such as the size of the market for a particular product in a particular country in one specific year) are converted into other currencies at the exchange rates that were valid at the time, in order be able to compare the various countries. We can thus compare, for example, the per capita beer consumption in different countries. It then appears as if beer consumption has been increasing rapidly over the last few years. In reality, though, Europeans are drinking less and less beer.

> The statistic shows an exchange rate effect. Only use such data if the figures have been converted using constant exchange rates (the same exchange rate for every year, such as today's rate), if they are given in local currencies or, even better, if they use data relating to volumes (litres instead of euros) and inflation.

- Do we not perhaps base ourselves too much on a statistical world? If the analysis indicates that the company is changing while the rest of the world remains the same, ask whether this is probable.

- Are the known ratios correct? If the analysis shows a change in certain ratios it can be an indication that something is wrong. If the wage costs per unit drop dramatically, there must be a reason for it. If we see a sharp decline in sales costs per unit of turnover, it means that there is something going on.

- Are we making any senseless calculations? If the company achieves a net margin of 2% there isn't much sense in forecasting the future margin by modelling costs and earnings. After all, it only takes a 1% fluctuation in either of the two factors (and that is at the very least conceivable) for us to be 50% out in calculating the margin.

Pitfall: overestimating synergy

A merger or a takeover can be attractive if there is synergy. The companies are then worth more together because they can do more or because they can do the same thing more cheaply. It is thus important when setting the price to estimate the values of the various advantages. Then these advantages must be realised. Recent history shows that it is not easy to achieve the value that was calculated beforehand.

Overestimating advantages of scale

An important source of synergy is to exploit the effects of scale. The average costs per unit decrease as the number of units increases. However, people are often rather optimistic about the advantages or forget that it also takes some effort to realise these advantages.

Example: As soon as two organisations merge, they only need one board of directors, one human resources department and so on. As a result, fixed overheads as a percentage of turnover should decrease. But are these overheads quite so fixed? That would mean that large companies have lower overheads on average than comparable smaller companies. In reality these sorts of savings prove to be rather hard to achieve. A significant part of the supposedly fixed overheads is in fact very variable in character.

Example: The development, implementation and maintenance of administrative systems cost banks (to take one example) a lot of money. When two banks join together they can save part of these costs. It makes no sense to develop systems twice and twice as much data will fit into such a system. There is a great temptation to put one lot of system development costs on the books as undeviating savings. However, in doing this you forget that a one-off investment is needed to make the two data structures fuse in such a way that they fit into the same system. Take these investments into consideration.

Overestimating the commercial advantages

A further source of synergy can be found in the commercial domain, as a result of cross-selling, for instance. If a hardware wholesaler and a packaging manufacturer merge they can sell each other's products to their customers. Here, too, excessive optimism can lead to disappointment. Are buyers of hardware really such active users of packaging and, if so, will they switch to a new supplier? If they now buy from a competitor, won't they have good reasons for doing so? In those cases where switching suppliers really doesn't cost the customer anything, we are often talking about a commodity, for which price is the deciding factor. Someone who counts on considerable added value through cross-selling runs the risk of thinking themselves rich without actually being so. Check the cross-selling expectations with those customers with whom you expect the effects to be strongest.

Step 4   Force the team to reach a conclusion

There is a general idea that the question can only be answered once the analysis is completely finished, but that is usually not the case. The question is: 'Can the remainder of the analysis alter the answer to the question or the outcome of the checks?' If the answer is no, why should we complete the analysis? Force the team to draw conclusions as soon as they can, by regularly attempting to formulate a conclusion, then testing whether it can be supported by evidence. Take a situation where the logistical analysis is not quite finished because a few minor expenses still need to be checked. The analysis so far reveals a large discrepancy between the optimal costs and the actual costs. The team's conclusion that it is possible to do things more cheaply would therefore appear to be justified. Does it still make sense to delve deeply into these left-over details? Probably not.

Force yourself towards conclusions using questions such as:

- If I met a member of the board in the lift and they asked me what our conclusions were likely to be, what would I say? In consultancy firms this is known as the *elevator pitch.*

- If I fill in the most likely results for the details that are still missing, what would the conclusion be then? And how likely are outcomes that are completely different from the most probable ones?

Step 5   Think about the *so what* question

The *so what* question is perhaps the best-known consulting concept after the 80/20 rule. It refers to the need to ask yourself this question for each conclusion. What do we learn from this conclusion, why is this conclusion important, what does it mean for the final conclusion, and what are we going to do with it now? Anticipate possible questions and reactions from stakeholders to the conclusion.

Hat or walking stick?

Suppose our company organises boat tours on the Danube. We don't need to do much research to establish that the overwhelming majority of our customers will be older people. So what? Is that positive, because if we look at the statistics the number of elderly people is set to rise in most western countries? Or is it negative as, looking at the statistics again, our customers are likely to die over the coming years? This depends on whether boat trips on the Danube are the domain of those we will refer to as the 'hat wearers' or those we can call the 'walking stick carriers'. Wearing a hat is a feature of a particular *generation*. As this generation dies out, hats disappear from the streets. Using a walking stick is closely linked to *age*. As more and more people reach a certain age, more walking sticks appear on the streets.

An uneven age distribution can thus have different effects. Find out whether the product or service is a hat or a walking stick. In other words, do these cruises on the Danube appeal to a generation that has never travelled very far and finds such a boat trip exciting enough, whereas future generations, accustomed to exotic holidays, will turn their noses up at such tame fare? Conversely, does this sort of trip appeal to an age group that is a bit shaky on its pins and cannot manage other types of holidays? The answer can only be found by means of a customer analysis. If the customers are purely hats it means that the average age of the consumer increases by a year each year. This does not hold true if they are purely walking sticks (leaving aside an increase in life expectancy). The motives of the two groups also differ.

Make sure that the team members continually ask themselves and each other the *so what* question. In a team in which the subsidiary questions and the analyses are divided up between the team members, and in which the members often tend to busy themselves with their own bits of work, the *so what* question provides a good excuse for a group discussion. In this way the team members are involved in other parts of the project and thus the connections become clearer for everyone.

Say the company has been able to maintain its total share of the market. An analysis shows that we lose market share with smaller business clients and gain market share with the larger accounts. Moreover, our margin appears to be rather limited with the smaller customers. What should we do about it? Is this situation favourable (we are gaining ground where the margin is highest) or unfavourable (we are only performing as regards market share and margin in an area that is quite possibly attractive to other parties in the market)? Should we concentrate particularly on our larger customers?

The *so what* question leads to follow-up questions. Why are we actually losing ground with smaller clients? Which players do well out of smaller clients and do they make a profit in that segment? What do those players do differently from us? Are the differences structural? If not, are we at a disadvantage when it comes to the smaller clients because we do not concentrate on them exclusively, or should we rather make the most of the fact that we also serve the big accounts? In other words, shouldn't we be able to grow well in the small customer segment with a different product or service concept?

Step 6   Set your sights on end products

Without end products there is no result. However, it is not everyone's natural tendency to use the result of an analysis or discussion immediately to create a relevant end product that is accessible to all. You carry out an analysis, you discover something, you get a glimmer of a higher understanding of the situation, there is a moment of euphoria, you can see a series of logical steps before you, and so on. At that point, few people will have the patience to sit down with a notepad in order to set down the results of the analysis, show the underpinning and the sources of information, then test the whole to make sure it is clear and to catch possible errors (see Figure 9.1).

However, every insight must be translated directly into an end product, for two reasons. First, knowledge and understanding that are inside somebody's head are of no use to a team. A team can only function as such if every person's knowledge is made available to the other team members. Second, it will be a very hard task to deliver an end product

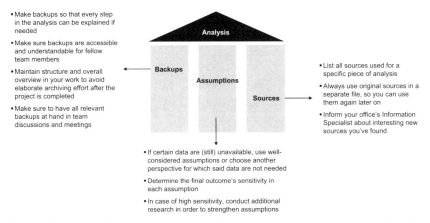

- Make backups so that every step in the analysis can be explained if needed
- Make sure backups are accessible and understandable for fellow team members
- Maintain structure and overall overview in your work to avoid elaborate archiving effort after the project is completed
- Make sure to have all relevant backups at hand in team discussions and meetings

Analysis

Backups

Assumptions

Sources

- List all sources used for a specific piece of analysis
- Always use original sources in a separate file, so you can use them again later on
- Inform your office's Information Specialist about interesting new sources you've found

- If certain data are (still) unavailable, use well-considered assumptions or choose another perspective for which said data are not needed
- Determine the final outcome's sensitivity in each assumption
- In case of high sensitivity, conduct additional research in order to strengthen assumptions

Figure 9.1 No analysis is complete without careful documentation of background material, sources and assumptions

when the whole project is finished if nothing has been produced in the interim.

An end product can be, among other things, an interview report, a list, a table, a graph or a sketch of the market structure. The fundamental point is that an end product must provide a conclusion. This does not yet have to be a complete answer to one of the subsidiary questions but, one way or another, you must draw a conclusion that is relevant to the subsidiary questions. If it is not possible to draw a conclusion it means that the analysis was unnecessary or that it is not yet complete.

Step 7   Revise the work plan where necessary

During the preparation phase the team drew up a work plan, based on what was known at the time. The questions and hypotheses from that phase form the basis for the analyses.

New insights, however, can have consequences for the work plan.

Suppose that one of the subsidiary questions concerns the development of products for the hobby market. The analyses relating to another subsidiary question have already shown, however, that the possibilities for gaining access to the appropriate distribution channels for the hobby market are very limited. This analysis has also shown that the channel for small business customers is not only easy to access but that there is lively demand from that segment for a number of suitable products. It is clear that the work plan must be adjusted. Instead of looking at the hobby market we should research whether we can build up a position in the small business market.

Do not be too sparing with revisions to the work plan. It is pointless to finish something just because it is in the plan. Changes in views lead to changes in the work plan. The previously mentioned *so what* discussions are particularly apt to bring about changes in the route taken. This does not have to cause extra work as certain analyses can sometimes be dropped.

Step 8 Monitor progress

Be careful – the analysis phase has a tendency to expand. There is a danger of irrelevant analyses being added to the list. Somebody thinks that you *always* have to have a SWOT analysis, a market analysis or a 'whatever else' analysis. Other excuses are that somebody thinks that something would 'just be nice to know', or that everybody has forgotten what the question actually was. Be disciplined. If an analysis doesn't help to find an answer to a question, it is superfluous.

Half way through there is a danger that some of the analyses will not be ready on time. The data were slow in coming, the model showed some very strange results, the team members had less time than expected or interview candidates were not available in time. Luckily there is always a lot of 'give' in a work plan, at the level of abstraction, in the amount of precision and in the available team capacity. Look for ways of completing the work plan in the time available after all:

- *Stay at a slightly higher level of abstraction*

  Someone who is contemplating introducing a new product category can try to estimate the total media mix and promotion costs. However, at this stage an estimate of the total advertising and promotion budget needed will probably suffice.

- *Sacrifice some precision*

  The person who wants to compare their prices with those of the competition can comb through all the supermarket chains in the country, but a carefully chosen sample may also suffice.

- *Delegate work to others*

  It is a huge amount of work for the team to find out which direct competitors are established within a radius of 250 km of each of our shops, but it is just the thing for the property manager.

10

Days 43 to 45 – We present the conclusions

What is the goal for these days?

The analysis phase is at an end. By now the team understands what is going on, where the opportunities lie, what general moves are worth thinking about and how we can beat the competitor at their own 'game'. In the worst case scenario the rest of the world knows nothing about all this. In the best case there has been contact with the steering committee before now.

The steering committee must now be informed about the team's findings and conclusions. This is not in order to make a choice about the future of the company as no choices are as yet being offered, but rather to create a general understanding of what is going on. Then, in the next phase, it will be possible to think about strategic options.

We describe below a few steps you can take to engage in discussion with the steering committee. Some of them are not really appropriate for this advanced stage of the project but we have included them in order to give a more thorough overview of reporting techniques. These may be of some support for those who may be involved in interim reports and brainstorming sessions. What are possible steps?

Step 1   Establish the aims of communication

A presentation to the steering committee quickly conjures up an image of a talk using all sorts of pictures – graphs, histograms and lots of snazzy arrows and circles. The well-known consultant's presentation. If only we could draw such lovely pictures!

But this is not about a lot of pretty pictures, it is about a story, an argument. The nature of the story depends on the aim of the session (see Figure 10.1). What are the team's aims for this session with the steering committee? There are all sorts of different possible aims, which fit in with the different stages of the project.

Testing the findings

In many cases the team will want to hear from the steering committee whether the findings are correct so far. The steer-

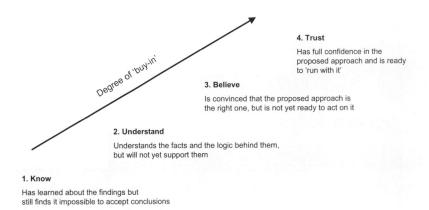

Figure 10.1 Gradually building the steering committee's 'buy-in'

ing committee members are of course often people who know the company and the sector well. They have something to contribute.

Requesting guidance

In some cases the team may head off in two very different directions, both of which could have significant consequences for the strategy. In this case it can make sense to discuss the choice of direction with the steering committee.

Previewing the findings

A strategic investigation quite often throws up a number of surprises, sometimes rather unpleasant ones. It is a good idea to let the steering committee members get used to the bad news gradually. You can say things like: 'That product that is selling so well – it turns out that, well, unfortunately we aren't making as much profit on it as we thought,' or: 'It looks as if selling the division is the only way to achieve a positive cash flow.' Previewing the results works best when the findings are not yet final as the messages are then less threatening.

Generating ideas

A session with the steering committee can supply a whole heap of ideas. In order to gauge the steering committee's agenda and expectations and, at the same time, to get a lot of ideas quickly, it is advisable to organise such a session early in the project timetable.

Convincing the committee

If the steering committee doesn't support the findings it might be necessary to hold a session to convince them. This is particularly the case when there are findings that are new to the committee. It is too optimistic to spring something completely new on the steering committee and expect the members to be converted immediately, in the same session. In many cases it is a mistake to push too hard in the first session. You run the risk that the committee members just dig in their heels and refuse to be swayed from a particular standpoint. Put off the discussion until later and hold a persuading session.

Step 2   Prepare the story

You then have to prepare your arguments. Pull together all the findings as a good story will have one overarching message

– the synthesis. A story without a message is not only a waste of time, it is also dead boring and not a good advertisement for the team's work.

What is this overarching message that emerges from the various findings? Formulate the real strategic messages. This is a creative, *inductive* process:

- First, write down all the findings and/or conclusions, preferably on one sheet of paper.

- Group together findings that are connected in order to uncover one major line of reasoning.

- Express this line of reasoning in strategically relevant terms.

Develop a storyline, or structure, to underpin or explain the overarching message. There are various different ways of structuring a story.

The linear story

This is the style that most resembles a graduation thesis. It starts with the framework of the investigation, then gives the results and the conclusions, and finally presents the recommendations. The advantage is that one can see the recommendations coming and that, by the time the recommendations are presented, the listeners have already heard the supporting evidence. The disadvantage is that for a large part of the presentation you bombard your audience with supporting material but the audience doesn't know *what* all this evidence is supposed to support. The conclusions and recommendations have not yet been mentioned. As a result the listeners do not properly take in the arguments. Leading strategy consultancies seldom use this type of presentation structure.

The 'walk in the woods'

In this type of talk the speaker presents a series of apparently unconnected messages without at this stage drawing any overarching conclusions. This style is well suited to testing and previewing preliminary findings. The steering committee may perhaps start to formulate conclusions itself, which would considerably increase the likelihood of the conclusions being accepted.

Writing according to the Minto Pyramid Principle

A piece of business-related writing (a memo, a letter, a report or a presentation) is normally required to deliver an action-orientated message in a short and snappy way. This can be a bit of a challenge if the message has to be gleaned from a pile of analyses. With the help of the 'Minto Pyramid Principle', the team can effectively and efficiently select the information needed, for instance, for a report or a presentation to the steering committee. The Minto Pyramid Principle helps the team to move from analysis to communication. The first thing to do is to think carefully: What is our message and how do we back it up?

This, briefly, is how to go about it. Work with a pencil and rubber. Take a blank sheet of paper and lay it down landscape fashion so that there is more space to write from left to right. Now write the main message of your piece at the top of the sheet, in the centre, in a single full sentence. In this sentence, the 'overarching message', we must explicitly define 'who', 'what' and 'why?'. For example:

- Our company . . . (who)

- . . . must purchase company X . . . (what)

- . . . in order to grow in market Y (why?).

The team must now work out which question this opening message will elicit from the steering committee: 'how' or 'why'? Choose the question that you expect and answer it on the next line in a few points – at most five or six. This second line of the plan is the *key line* – the main list of contents for the report or presentation. A *key line* for the *governing thought* mentioned above (the answer to the 'why?' question) might look like this:

- Market Y is an attractive growth market for our company

- Company X is a good springboard to Market Y

- Company X is in itself an attractive takeover target.

The team then once again chooses either the how or the why question for each of these three points. The answers appear on the next line of the plan. This question and answer game is repeated until there are sentences on the sheet of paper that will probably not prompt any more questions from the steering committee.

In this way you obtain a text structure that starts off narrow at the top, with the main message, then becomes steadily wider towards the base; hence the name 'pyramid principle'.[1]

This plan or outline contains all the building blocks needed for the main structure of the report or presentation: the *governing thought*, either shortened or left as it is, becomes the title, the sentences from the *key line*, either shortened or left as they are, become the chapter headings, and so on.

A pyramidal structure offers the team a bird's-eye view of the entire structure of the argument. The clear outline enables those involved, preferably working as a team, to check the quality of some important points in their intended argument before any part of the final text has been written:

- All the points clustered beneath an overarching message must answer one and the same imagined question: how or why?

- The sentences in the plan must progress from the more abstract at the top to the more concrete at the

[1] Freely adapted from: Minto, B. (1996). *The Minto Pyramid Principle: Logic in Writing, Thinking and Problem Solving*. London: Minto.

bottom. In other words, going from the bottom to the top, the points contained in each horizontal cluster are 'synthesised' in the overarching message.

- Each (horizontal) cluster of points beneath an overarching message must be MECE – Mutually Exclusive, Collectively Exhaustive, i.e. there must be no overlap and no gaps in the series of points. 'Apples – pears – other fruit' is MECE, 'apples – pears – golden delicious' is not.

Finally: an effective pyramid structure stands or falls with the quality of the individual sentences. To achieve this you must write the sentences out carefully and completely. Bear in mind the fact that a perfect structure does not exist. The Minto Pyramid Principle is a tool with which the team first forces itself to think carefully about logic and phrasing before writing the text.

The conclusion-orientated story

With this structure the speaker presents the overarching message, that is to say the synthesis, right at the beginning of the talk. The rest of the presentation is a systematic, point-by-point defence of the conclusions given. Advantages of this style are that the overarching message cannot be missed and that the logic of the story is brought to the fore. The data and analyses serve strongly to underpin the conclusions. A disadvantage is that listeners who have no prior knowledge of the messages may feel rather overwhelmed by this direct style. Difficult messages can alienate the audience and cause the listeners to switch off, with the result that all the arguments fall on deaf ears. This structure is suitable for the presentation of a complete and carefully considered story, for which the audience has been properly prepared with previews of the outcomes. A structure that is often used for this kind of storyline is the pyramid structure (see box for a brief explanation).

So now you must choose a form to use. This leads us back to the matter of the 'pictures'. Is a talk with projected slides, where one person stands up and presents something while the rest of the company sits and listens, a suitable structure? Not for every purpose and every storyline (see Figure 10.2). Weigh up the various possibilities:

- The presentation delivered standing up and using slides projection to back up the arguments is particularly appropriate for a formal final presentation to a fairly large audience. This form of talk does not automatically stimulate discussion as the person at the head of the table always has the floor. If a discussion is wanted it has to be ex-

Methods for improving client 'buy-in'	Communication format	Impact on decision-makers
Inform the steering committee about the findings	Presentations	Attention
Involve the steering committee in addressing specific issues	Discussion sessions	Answers, ideas
Have the steering committee contribute to solving issues	Workshops; team working sessions	Ideas, commitment
Share concerns with the steering committee	Personal relationships	Emotions, trust

Figure 10.2 A formal presentation isn't the only possible communication format

plicitly programmed into the presentation. A discussion can be part of the agenda, perhaps with a list of the questions or viewpoints to be discussed.

- The sit-down presentation, where the participants go over a number of slides on paper together, is more suited to a smaller group. This setting also invites greater participation from those present. However, such a set-up is still rather formal in character.

- A conversational setting is a very good way of testing preliminary findings or previewing results. The results are not yet definitive and the threshold for taking part in the discussion is low. One disadvantage is that it is difficult to communicate complicated concepts and enumerations. The team can perhaps bring in a number of essential graphs as supporting material, which they can use where necessary.

- The workshop, in which the participants actively take part, can provide ideas and insights (see Figure 10.3). In

	Interim presentation	Workshop
Mode of thought	Convergent	Divergent
Characteristics	Many findings/conclusions	Many issues
Typical agenda	• Agreeing on analysis • Discussing findings/conclusions • Agreeing on work plans	• Generating ideas • Determining options • Developing market insights
Content on paper	A lot	Little
Style of chairing the meeting	• Semi-formal • Issue-resolving	• Informal • Consensus is not a goal

Figure 10.3 Interim reports and workshops: different objectives

terms of problem solving this is a much more productive format than a standard (interim) presentation. What is more, a workshop makes the participants feel more involved. This format is, however, not suitable for a rounding-off phase or when conclusions need to be tested or approved. A workshop throws the discussion open completely and generates new tasks for the team.

Step 3   Design the slides

In many cases it is a good idea to use some slides to aid communication. These can support certain core messages or clarify a difficult concept. Make a slide in three stages (see Figure 10.4).

Decide on the message

A good slide always contains a conclusion that is relevant to the central question. A slide without a conclusion makes no sense. Slides without conclusions lead to the maddening piles of tables and graphs mentioned previously, which tell us nothing. The first step in making a slide is to decide on the message. What do we want to say? A message on a slide is always (1) clear, (2) true and (3) relevant:

- *Clear*

   Limit yourself to one message per slide. Put this message at the top of the page. The main message is thus not 'profit development per region' but rather 'profit on exports down to zero in a few years'. Make sure that the audience does

Generic approach to visualising findings

Strongly simplified

Decide on the message	Choose the logic	Visualise
▪ Conclusion-orientated (not: 'the market')	▪ In line with the message	▪ Visual expresses the message
▪ One clear-cut message (per visual)	▪ Convincing 'proof'	▪ In line with the supporting logic
▪ Fitting with the context of the story	▪ Clearly reasoned	▪ Clearly recognisable

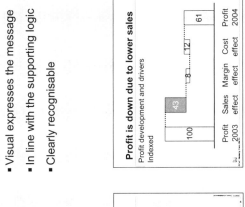

Figure 10.4 Developing effective diagrams – three steps

not have to search for the main message in a profusion of circles and boxes that clutter the screen. If this happens, the message is lost in a sea of illustrations, whereas the illustrations were meant precisely to emphasise the message.

- *True*

  Not all evidence has to be completely hard but make sure that the facts are real facts.

- *Relevant*

  To make sure that the slide provides support in answering a question, it is sensible to look for the right graph to go with the message, not the message to fit the graph. If you first sketch out a graph and then think what the message is, it is difficult to come to a relevant message. If you first consider what message you want to communicate, you can then sketch the appropriate graph. Adapting the facts to fit the desired message is of course not the intention.

Decide on the logic that needs to be presented in graphic form

A slide is based on a particular logic, a line of reasoning. What does it tell our audience if we say that the market share of multinational retail chains in the toy market is 23%? This fact only has meaning if you also know that this market share was just 14% three years ago, or that this share is already at 45% in countries with a more developed market. This logic can be the same as that which formed the basis for the analysis. Below are a few commonly used slide types:

- The *share graph* shows what share something is of the whole, such as the sales costs as a proportion of total costs (one-dimensional) or our company's share of the whole market, divided according to submarkets.

- The *time series* shows developments over time of, for example, turnover or results.

- The *comparison* demonstrates how a value (e.g. advertising costs per inhabitant) relates to the same value in other markets, other situations and so on.

- The *correlation* shows what kind of connection exists between two variables, for example the link between the number of television sets per household and disposable income per household.

- The *explanation of a change* or of a difference shows how a change in a variable (such as last year's profit as against profit five years ago) can be explained, or how the difference between two variables (such as our unit costs versus those of our competitor) can be explained. Which cause is responsible for which part of the difference?

Choose the most appropriate graphic form

It must support the chosen logic and underline the message. Don't make the slides too difficult to read. Use large enough type and don't put the information in a separate key, as this can turn the whole thing into a puzzle. Simply write the details next to the relevant sections. Here are a few general recommendations:

Sales by product and market – 2002
(%)

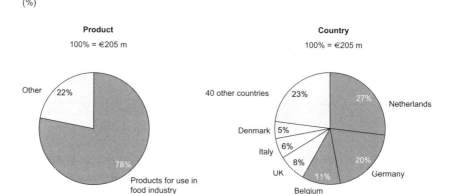

Figure 10.5 X mainly sells supplements for the food industry in the Benelux countries and Germany

- A *pie chart* is good for indicating a share (see Figure 10.5) but it is less suitable if we want to show the development of that share over time. Who is capable of rapidly comparing the sizes of the various pie slices on different pie charts?

- A *bar or column graph* is used to show developments or comparisons. For a comparison we use a slide with horizontal bars placed one above the other (see Figure 10.6). For a time series we use a slide with vertical columns standing next to each other (see Figure 10.7). This is because people automatically interpret a horizontal comparison as a development over time. To show the development in a share we again use a slide with vertical columns ranged next to each other (after all, it is a time series), where the columns are divided into sections in order to show the different shares (see Figure 10.8).

Media expenditure and market share – Italy, 2001

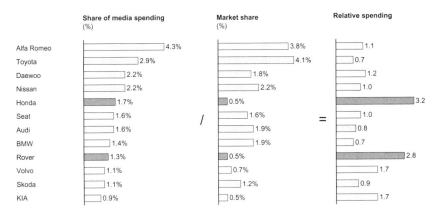

Source: Nielsen Media Research; OC&C analysis

Figure 10.6   Honda and Rover's spending on media is relatively high

Growth projections by segment, 2003F–2008F
(€m)

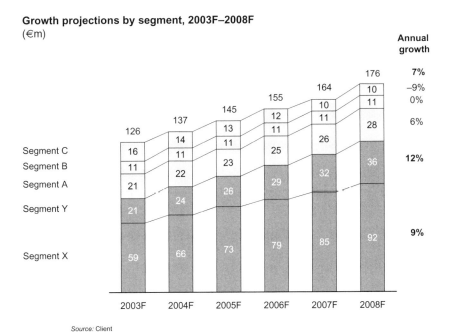

Source: Client

Figure 10.7   Strong growth expected in the use of our product in segment X and Y

EU markets for animal food supplements, projections (ktonne)

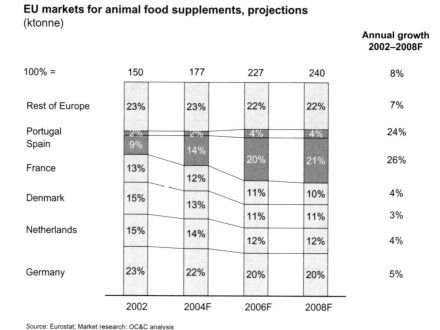

Source: Eurostat; Market research: OC&C analysis

Figure 10.8 Spain and Portugal's shares of total market expected to rise sharply

- A *line graph* is useful for showing a time series but it can also be used for correlations (see Figure 10.9). Make sure that the 'independent variable' (or the most likely candidate) is on the horizontal axis.

- A *waterfall* (see Figure 10.10) is used to interpret variations between two values.

- A *map plot* (see Figure 10.11) indicates a share in a two-dimensional whole, for example different breweries' shares of the total beer market, divided according to types of beer.

Sales development by sales point
(number of units)

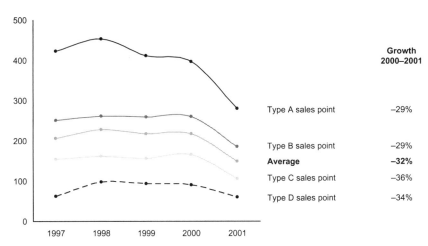

Figure 10.9   All sales points reported a sharp drop in sales following introduction of a new strategy

Sales development in Russia, 2004–2006
(€m)

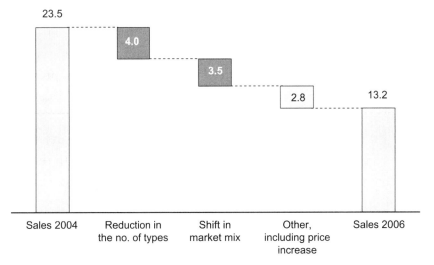

Figure 10.10   Sharp sales drop is due mainly to the reduction in number of types and shift in market mix – less to price increase

Shares of beer market, country A – 2005
(%)

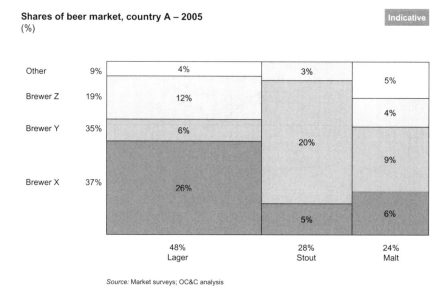

Source: Market surveys; OC&C analysis

Figure 10.11 Brewers X and Y have similar overall market share but are focused on different segments

Step 4   Give the presentation

The day of the presentation arrives. Everyone has already done a presentation course at some time and we are not going to repeat that here. As a rule, though, it is not the presentation techniques that we need to watch the most:

- Leave time for discussion and reflection. Make sure that the steering committee members don't have to run out of the room immediately after the presentation to get to another appointment.

- Undertake follow-up steps for the most controversial points. Is there a need for a persuasion session? Do we need to talk to some of the committee members separately?

- Include on the agenda an opportunity for making follow-up appointments. Don't end up with a feeling of 'what now?'.

- Listen actively and make notes. No steering committee member will think that they are being listened to if the team members, exhausted after all the hard work, sit slumped at the table and fail to note down any remarks. Have pen and paper in hand and look alert!

- Keep background data and explanations at the ready. Ensure that team members who have carried out specific, complex analyses are present.

- If you get bogged down on particular points, leave them until a later date. Prevent team members or steering committee members from digging in their heels on any points, as in 'I think we need to have another good look at the analysis of market growth. Can we ask the marketing director about it sometime soon?'

And with that, the analysis phase is finished. We know what we need to know. Now it comes down to choices. On to the next phase.

11

Allware: on with the analysis

RELIEVED THAT SCHMIDT HAS GIVEN HIS BLESSING TO her focused, problem-driven approach, Jenny has got to work with a number of *high potentials* from different countries' organisations and the group controller. The team is enthusiastic because, as a young employee, when do you get the chance to analyse your own company so thoroughly and – you hope – to change it for the better? The fact that Schmidt regularly joins the team meetings of course boosts motivation even further.

Each of the team members has been allocated a part of the question tree. Each of them must look for possibilities of increasing market share in one of the three sectors that are most under pressure: petrochemicals (where Allware seems to be failing to keep up with the trend towards long-lasting, exclusive key supplier relationships with clients), the heating market (where Allware risks losing its wholesale channel) and the offshore sector (where Allware's price level appears to be structurally too high). Each one of them will have their own 'eureka' moments and come up against their own hurdles, as we shall see below.

Petrochemicals: key suppliership is worthwhile

Rodrik Mathews thinks that he has been given a pretty easy task, when he compares his with that of the others. The question tree offers quite a lot of guidance in the search for a solution and the hypothesis is very strong: key suppliership is the trend in the petrochemicals industry and Allware must follow that trend. It's odd that Allware didn't start doing this long ago.

'I'd like to,' says Rodrik's boss in answer to his question, 'but I'm not allowed to. Margins on key suppliership contracts are far too low. They are below our minimum norms. And clients nearly always ask for more than just valves and gaskets. They often want us to start running product groups such as security equipment or lubricants for them, although we have no buying power at all in those areas. The challenge is to find a way to achieve profitable key suppliership relationships.'

Rodrik doesn't understand. 'But surely our competitors aren't crazy? They go along with these demands, so how do they do it?'

'I think they go a bit crazy at the tendering stage,' says his boss. 'After all, large contracts over many years are at stake and they are afraid of losing them. Maybe in a few years' time they will stop doing this, then prices will rise again and we will be able to join in.'

Naturally Rodrik does not want to wait this long. He is not quite so sure that it is really impossible to earn money with these contracts. Luckily he was a management accountant in his former life, so he can be entrusted with a substantial financial analysis. The analysis reveals that margins are indeed low, but the costs of arranging a key suppliership contract are also low. After all, the contracts are for large quantities, with high delivery predictability. Thus stocks can be kept low and Allware should be in a position to negotiate favourable conditions with its own suppliers for the (relatively small and specialised) range of products. When you work them out thoroughly, the contracts aren't at all as unattractive as at first sight. There is of course still the matter of the additional product ranges, but Jenny has a solution for that problem. 'Why don't we bring in one of our purchasing managers? Let them get in touch with suppliers of security equipment, for example. Maybe they would be interested in working with us.'

Rodrik's analysis of the real profitability of key suppliership contracts has some repercussions. Inspired by Rodrik's work, the group controller decides to carry out a substantial analysis of Allware's profitability in all segments.

He calculates the costs anew on the basis of the characteristics and cost drivers of the different market segments. This not only confirms Rodrik's calculations, it also brings to light a new conclusion. Allware attributes a disproportionate share of costs to the shipping sector. Is that perhaps the reason that the contract with Pantagruel Shipbuilding was lost? Is Allware pricing itself out of the market?

The heating market: fighting your own customers for the market

Isabelle Tobur has been working in France for two years now. Together with a German colleague, she has been given the task of understanding why the company's share of the heating market is shrinking in both countries. The products (a wide range of connectors, thermostats, gaskets and valves under the trade name Allheat) are sold through regional wholesalers who sell the products on to their customers (small, independent heating engineers). Allware is finding it more and more difficult to maintain its exclusive relationships with the independent wholesalers, in spite of the excellent reputation of its brand with heating engineers and its very full product range. The wholesalers are buying some products ever more frequently from Allware's competitors and sometimes even introduce their own, non-branded products. So far none of them has completely turned their back on Allware but the company's market share with its own clients (that is to say the share of the heating equipment range that they buy from Allware) has declined to 74% from 83% in just three years.

Isabelle's own boss does not offer her much inspiration. 'It's just that we are no longer unique in the market. Previously we were the only ones who could supply the wholesale market, but now there are a few local players who offer a range that is nearly as broad as ours. It's logical that the wholesalers make room on their shelves for the other products. Nobody likes a monopoly. It's lucky that the heating engineers still believe in the Allheat brand, otherwise things would be even worse for us.'

Is her boss right and is a decline unavoidable? How can she come up with ideas to reverse the downward trend? If she can't find ideas in her own immediate surroundings, she might have to look for them in completely different markets.

Isabelle discovers that in other wholesale markets suppliers of branded goods often have their own, more direct distribution to the end consumer. In the distribution of, for instance, electronic components, fasteners and technical lubricants, it is very common for companies to maintain their own networks of sales points. These service centres only supply the companies' own brands, sometimes with the addition of some items from other product groups. The look and feel of these service centres is thus wholly centred around the companies' own brands.

Isabelle visits some of these service centres and interviews local managers. It is very noticeable that these people talk about their products with a lot of enthusiasm and detailed knowledge. Isabelle also notices that customers come and go, but that they also often hang around for a while to chat with each other or with members of staff at the centrally placed table where people can have a cup of coffee.

'But don't your customers want to have a choice of different brands or a range that is much broader than just nuts and screws?' she asks the manager of a Bolts centre specialising in fasteners.

'What our customers want,' the manager explains, 'is good advice and the certainty that the product can do what they want it to do. The price is a lot less important, as the cost of materials is nothing compared with labour costs. What our customers also want is a meeting place where they can discuss the latest developments with colleagues.'

As Isabelle is driving home after this interview she spots another service centre belonging to the same manufacturer. On closer inspection, however, it turns out to be an independent wholesaler who has adopted the same look and feel and offers exclusively the Bolts range of products.

A few weeks later Isabelle has another talk with her boss. She has prepared well and has done her sums. 'What we need to do,' she says, 'is to bring a superior alternative to the independent wholesaler on to the market. It should be an Allheat service centre with well-trained staff who can explain precisely to the heating engineers which valve they should use under what conditions. They should also have contacts with building firms and property developers so that they can point the engineers in the direction of new contracts. Allheat is still *the* brand in the heating market. Let's make use of that strength. My model calculations show that we would earn almost as much from distributing our products through our own service centres as we do through independent wholesalers, but without the risk of losing market share!'

Unfortunately her boss is not very convinced. 'But that's suicide,' he says. 'How do you think our wholesale customers are going to react to that? They'll go straight over to another supplier.'

Isabelle is ready for this objection. 'That's why we must open such service centres first of all in areas where we don't have good distribution at present, or where our market share is already very low. If we can prove there that the concept works we can convince the wholesalers that they have to work with us. They will become Allheat centres, with all the advantages that that brings. That's the beauty of it. If we can show that we can introduce a superior alternative to the independent wholesalers on to the market, the wholesalers will go along with us purely in order to survive.'

The offshore sector: organising for projects

Thorsten Lundvik has come from the offshore business. He knows it as a market where trustworthiness and quality are all important and price is a secondary consideration. After working for Allware for a couple of months he therefore doesn't understand the opinion of his boss at all. According to his boss: 'We are just too expensive and we lose on price.' 'That can't be true,' thinks Thorsten and he decides to calculate the relative importance of the price of Allware products in a typical offshore installation. And yes indeed, he finds what he expected: it is less than 1% of the costs of the drilling platform. Thus price cannot be important. He will go and reassure his boss with this information and at the same time prove the value of a fresh pair of eyes.

However, his boss is not impressed: 'Those model calculations are all very well, but shouldn't you go and actually ask our clients.' Thorsten decides to call those customers with whom Allware has lost tenders recently. To his surprise the unanimous response is 'too expensive'. 'But surely it's only a matter of a relatively small amount?' he counters. 'Yes,' says the customer, 'but all things considered it's still a couple of million. So it's worth our while to let a project buyer spend a few weeks on it.'

So his boss was right after all. But why is Allware too expensive? It is one of the largest suppliers of these sorts of products worldwide, so the problem cannot have anything to do with buying power. Thorsten has learned from his mistake of trying to answer questions from behind his desk. He puts together a small working group with a sales representative, a buyer and a logistics manager. Together they analyse the whole process and together they arrive at surprising conclusions. It is not so inexplicable that Allware is expensive. In the offshore sector a big project only comes along every now and then. At that point the seller is very busy but for the rest of the time he can't actually do very much. In the long periods between infrequent projects Allware's products sit gathering dust in the warehouse. These are expensive products from expensive European and US quality suppliers.

Jenny is very enthusiastic when she hears about this analysis: 'We must organise this business internationally, with international account managers who fly from country to country so that they can always be occupied with a project. And we'll buy the products from China. After all, we know well in advance when we need to deliver what. That gives us plenty of time to have things produced in China to our specifications and have them certificated in Europe. That would get rid of those expensive supplies straight away.'

An unruly presentation

Jenny has been looking forward to presenting all these findings to the steering committee. However, the presentation turns out to be the biggest disappointment of the project so far. While studying for her MBA Jenny learned to give the conclusions *up front*. That turns out to be a bad idea. When she projects her management summary on to the screen the objections begin: 'How can you just claim that? There isn't a single bit of evidence to support it,' says one committee member. 'Are you saying that I don't know my own business?' adds another. 'Have you discussed this with my account managers? I don't think any of this is true!' shouts a third. The shipping manager in particular is furious. Invited to the presentation at the last minute (so that he can be informed about the group controller's findings) he is unpleasantly surprised by what is being said about his pricing policy. 'Allware is kept afloat by the profits I make in my business unit. If you want me to lower my prices and push the whole company into the red, just say so. Maybe we can send our clients a cheque straight away to pay back all the excessive amounts that I've made them fork out over the years.'

Schmidt manages to get the meeting back on track to some extent, but nothing really constructive comes out of it any more. Jenny has made a serious error of judgement. Luckily Schmidt accepts some of the responsibility but he gives Jenny the task of immediately making appointments to speak to all the managers individually, to give them the opportunity of discussing their grievances with her.

Repairing the damage

During these individual sessions Jenny and her team are able to convince the managers of the quality of their work by taking them on a 'walk in the woods'. She goes through the analyses one by one, without drawing any very far-reaching conclusions. Luckily she can deliver a positive message: new opportunities for growth have been discovered. Together with the managers, Jenny formulates one conclusion for each division. Where necessary she arranges additional analyses. She also promises that in future she will first discuss her findings with each manager responsible before she presents them to the steering committee.

Part III – The decision-making phase

Introduction

A COMMON COMPLAINT OF TEAMS WHO HAVE WORKED on the strategy is: 'Those at the top did nothing with our work. They listened to it all then carried on with the order of the day. When are we actually going to define this new strategy?'

Those senior managers – they just can't make up their minds! Or is there perhaps something else going on? Senior managers must of course be prepared to make choices and for this to be possible the strategy teams must present some choices. Tracing out a strategy is *all about* making choices. Many teams fail to present their senior managers with clear options. There are lots of ideas; charts and diagrams race across the screen, but where are the options? And if there are options on the table, how can the heads of the company choose between them if the effects have not been quantified? Few senior managers are brilliant – or clairvoyant – enough to make the right choices on gut feeling alone.

We have already seen many possible choices fall by the wayside during the analysis phase. They were impossible, clearly unattractive or not distinctive enough. However, there are still options left in all sorts of areas. Some conflict with each other, others are complementary. There are in any case a limited number of possible directions to choose from and we cannot make a choice without looking at them more closely. In this last week we will use quantified, financial methods to weigh up the different directions and distinguish between them. We will then set the chosen option down in a strategic plan (see Figure III.1).

The structure of the book

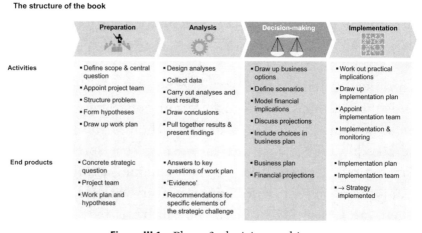

	Preparation	Analysis	Decision-making	Implementation
Activities	• Define scope & central question • Appoint project team • Structure problem • Form hypotheses • Draw up work plan	• Design analyses • Collect data • Carry out analyses and test results • Draw conclusions • Pull together results & present findings	• Draw up business options • Define scenarios • Model financial implications • Discuss projections • Include choices in business plan	• Work out practical implications • Draw up implementation plan • Appoint implementation team • Implementation & monitoring
End products	• Concrete strategic question • Project team • Work plan and hypotheses	• Answers to key questions of work plan • 'Evidence' • Recommendations for specific elements of the strategic challenge	• Business plan • Financial projections	• Implementation plan • Implementation team • → Strategy implemented

Figure III.1   Phase 3: decision-making

12

Day 46 – We put forward a few business options

What is our goal for today?

If you want to make a choice between different strategic directions you first need some directions to choose from. Today we are going to develop a limited number of distinctive and feasible strategic directions. We will describe each direction in the form of a business option: a mutually consistent collection of choices in specific areas, which together describe the company that we are aiming to create. This is a company with skills and production capacity, able to choose particular types of clients, products or services, and with the appropriate turnover and cost structure. We will determine these options today.

How do we go about it?

Step 1   Formulate the remaining options

In the preparation phase we formulated the central question by means of a number of subsidiary questions. Many of these subsidiary questions point to possible options. During the analysis phase the universe of choices shrank considerably as all sorts of possibilities turned out to be unattractive or unattainable. This simplifies the process as it is now clear what we should do with all the rejected choices: nothing. They do not offer us any help in formulating business options.

However, not every potential option is so obviously bad and before we put together our business options, we must properly understand the most important choices that remain. These represent different strategic directions which all appear to be feasible. We must use these directions to construct a number of internally consistent alternatives, which we must then compare with one another.

The brewer who wants to enter the market in a neighbouring country can do this in a number of ways. The analysis has perhaps shown that having its own cafés is not financially viable for the company. There remains the possibility of actively working existing cafés through a wholesaler, possibly with additional direct activities. Entering the market via the retail trade is also a possibility, which would require the brewer to work hard on the retailers and complement this activity with consumer advertising. These are all possibilities that have been elaborated and verified during the analyses. The brewer can start with its existing products for the domestic market, but sometimes a new product proposal is necessary to win over the customer. This can even be different for each channel. The brewer must also make choices about its organisational structure. Is it going to set up an export department or opt for a self-contained local operation? On top of that there are logistical choices to be made, and so on.

Keep only those options that will enable the company to 'win the game' one way or another. Work out why this particular option will allow us to beat our competitor. Will we be active in a different market segment, make a better product or do something unique that makes our costs structurally lower?

Pitfall: underestimating competitors' reactions

If we make that new product now, if we develop that new distribution channel now, if we now make that acquisition, if we now . . . then we will be too smart for the competition. That is true – if the competition does nothing. But some competitors do make a move. They copy us or they do something else clever. There is only a slim chance that today will mark a turning point in history, the day on which we gained a definitive lead on our rival. Look out for the following assumptions:

- A one-off improvement in our margin, which remains constant at the higher level without any extra effort.

- A one-off improvement in our market share, which remains constant at the higher level without any extra effort.

> This does not mean that improvements cannot lead temporarily to a better margin or higher turnover. Lasting improvements are rare, however. After us it is the competitor's turn again, which puts our margin or volume under pressure.

Step 2 Put together internally consistent options

We now have a number of remaining alternatives in different areas. Suppose we have two options left in the area of production, three for market development, two for distribution and we have four possible production configurations. In theory, then, there are 48 conceivable different business options. Are we going to work out 48 options and present them to the steering committee? Poor team – and poor steering committee!

Working out alternatives is not a purely mathematical activity. The combinations of possible choices *mean* something: they point towards a company that should be able to function in practice. On closer inspection some combinations turn out not to reflect the logic built up in the course of the analysis, or alternatively some combinations are internally inconsistent. Does an increased sales effort fit together with big savings in marketing expenses? Does a high level of service in the shops go together with prices at discount level? Does an advance in production methods fit with plans to outsource production? Does a functional structure fit with product diversification? The same answer fits all these questions: not under normal circumstances. So these alternatives are also dropped.

In this way the field of competing alternatives thins out very quickly. Aim to have a maximum of, say, four alternatives, but if there are four you should ask yourself whether all these alternatives really are quite so realistic. The existing organisation may in itself represent an outer limit for the strategy and thus partly determine what options are possible. Do we, for example, have the time and the skills ever to make this option a reality? If not, scrap that option.

Step 3   Describe the options in sufficient detail

The next step is to describe the alternatives, not only showing where they differ from one another but also making clear where they differ from the current situation. In order to model the alternatives, a number of facts must be determined. In the example of the brewer we must work out approximately how much turnover is expected per segment. What margin do we predict? What are the costs of the distribution channel? How much needs to be invested? Make clear where modelled alternatives originate. We cannot simply justify positive trends by saying that 'it must be possible'. Make clear what we are going to do differently from in the past and where the improvement is going to come from.

A large part of the company that is described in the different alternatives already exists. In most cases a new strategy is after all an addition to, or else a change in direction for, the current company. It is rare for a completely new company to be designed. Moreover, the alternatives must above all be specific as to the aspects where they deviate from the existing situation. Those aspects must be quite clear. You expect, for example, that for the brewery that is looking at a neighbouring country the alternatives offer clarification of the following questions:

- What is our proposition going to be and who is it for?

- Which client segments are we going to serve and to what extent? What needs are we going to satisfy?

- What product or service are we going to deliver? What will our product range be?

- What price levels are we going to use and what price differentiation are we going to apply?

- How are we going to produce and distribute the desired products?

- What type of production capacity do we have and how large is it? Where are we going to do our manufacturing and what processes and technology will we use? What is the cost structure of this?

- Which distribution channels are we going to use and to what extent? What is the cost structure of this?

Step 4   Rejig the company's orientation

The existing organisation (but also the position, the reputation, etc.) has so far represented a possible limit for the strategy, with the strategy partly following from the current organisation. At this stage we turn this around and ask what kind of organisation (skills, systems, structures) is necessary in order to be able to realise the strategy laid out in the various alternatives. To what extent can the current organisation adapt itself to the required profile? Are the existing employees, for example, capable of meeting the demands of the new strategy? Now it is the organisation that follows the strategy, within the bounds of possibility. Now that we have defined the options, we can set up an organisation for each one. This does not have to be done in great detail; we don't need an organisational chart to be able to choose between strategic alternatives. We only want to know roughly the size of the organisation for each alternative so as to be able to work out staff numbers and staffing costs.

At this stage we will also prepare a rough overview of the skills needed. To what extent does our current staff match the new situation or to what extent can it be made to fit in? How much investment in training and recruitment do we have to allow for? What level of costs for layoffs will we have to deal with?

Step 5   Give the options a distinctive label

Options are often combinations of choices in different areas. For an outsider who has not helped to put the options together it can be difficult to see what characterises a particular option and in what way the alternatives are distinguishable from one another. We must aid this recognition by giving each alternative a distinctive label, a descriptive name. The name is a synthesis of the underlying choices.

13

Day 47 – We set up scenarios

What is our goal for today?

We can control the things that we do ourselves but there is a lot going on in the world or in the market over which we have no influence. Some of these uncertainties have a great effect on our company's performance. They can even influence the choice between different options. If the oil price rises, if economic growth is favourable or if the law changes, this option becomes more attractive than the other.

For this reason we construct scenarios. Unlike options (don't get options mixed up with scenarios) scenarios contain elements that you as a company cannot fundamentally

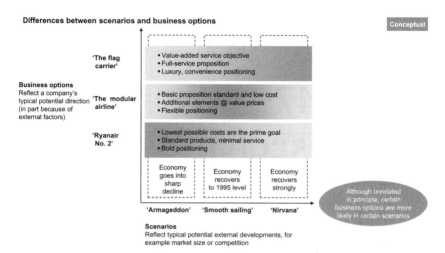

Figure 13.1   Scenarios and business options are *not* the same!

influence, but which *can* influence the choice between options (see Figure 13.1). Put briefly, a scenario describes what might *go on around* the company, an option describes what you as a company can *do*.

Today we construct the scenarios. How do we go about it?

Step 1   Identify the external uncertainties

The first step is to determine what circumstances can change without our company having any significant influence on them. We should look only at matters for which there is considerable uncertainty as to the outcomes and which have a fundamental influence on the company. For scenarios think about changes in the following areas.

Economy

Does the development of the economy have a great influence on the market? Is there a clear link to be found, for example, between consumption in the relevant sector and economic growth, or per capita GDP? Other macroeconomic parameters may also be important. The percentage of the population in work is a fundamental factor in public transport questions, while wage developments in relation to other countries are crucial to production activities.

Competition

Is the competitor expected to invest in new capacity or new technology? Can we expect more intense competition from foreign companies? What does this mean for the general price level and for capacity use in the sector?

Legislation

Do we expect the competitive position to be strongly influenced by changes in legislation, for example in the areas of working conditions, the environment, or by privatisation or deregulation, or in the area of subsidies?

Factor costs

Can we expect a lack of continuity in factor costs? Think of the development of the oil price. Such expectations are generally particularly meaningful if they are linked with developments in the competition or in alternatives.

Technology

Can we expect a new generation of technology that will make the current generation obsolete? What embryonic technologies can we identify? Is it already possible to see which technology has the best chance of becoming the new industry standard? Do we already know what this new technology will involve?

Step 2   Select uncertainties for the scenarios

Not all changes have to be expressed in the scenarios. Choose the most fundamental changes as the basis for the scenarios.

Uncertain scenario

Scenarios are all about uncertainties. If we already know how, to what extent and when the changes will take place, then those changes don't have to be part of a scenario. An example: demographic development considerably influences some business sectors, but the uncertainties are very limited as the expected change in population is known to within a reasonable margin. Thus, demographic change does not make a sensible basis for a scenario. Only if we can imagine distinctly different developments (the competitor either does or does not invest in a new factory) do we include them in a scenario.

Distinctive scenario

If the uncertainty, even taking into account the range of values that can be reasonably expected, has no great influence on the choice, then scenarios based on this uncertainty make little sense. This can have two causes. One is that the uncertainty has no great influence on the company's performance. For example, the oil price is a significant uncertainty but it has little influence on our brewer. In that case scenarios based on different oil prices make no sensible contribution. The other cause is that uncertainty influences the various different options to the same extent, so that the uncertainty has no effect on the choice.

Step 3   Construct internally consistent scenarios

Next we put together the scenarios. As with the options, we notice here too that not every possibility can be combined with every other possibility. The number of theoretical possibilities must be restricted to a small number of internally consistent scenarios. Would wage costs rise sharply in the case of disappointing economic growth? Would our competitor really make investments against a background of rapidly falling demand?

Focus on two or, at most, three scenarios, and then only if there are major external uncertainties. Avoid scenarios made up only of combinations of 'high', 'medium' and 'low' because the decision-maker then looks only at the 'medium' option, without knowing how to end up in the 'high' or 'low' situations. For preference make sure that scenarios are based on concrete events that better clarify the nature of the scenario, such as a rapid technological breakthrough that results in a drop in demand, excess capacity and a price war, or else a worldwide oil price escalation, resulting in slower economic growth, spiralling factor costs and a fall in investment.

Step 4   Translate the scenarios into consequences for the company

What do the scenarios mean for the company? Think about turnover, the cost position compared to competitors and the margin. Translate the unpredictable changes in the external, macroeconomic world into business economic consequences for the organisation.

Avoid scenarios in which purely positive or purely negative consequences are thoughtlessly thrown together. Make a meaningful translation of the imagined reality into model parameters. If, in a particular scenario, turnover declines, one can expect that working capital can also be reduced. In that case the consequences for cash flow are not necessarily all that unfavourable in the short term.

14

Days 48 to 57 – We model the results

What is the goal for these days?

We cannot expect senior management to reach a decision about the future of the organisation without having a sound understanding of the financial consequences. To that end we model the financial outcomes of the different alternatives. However, a good financial model offers more advantages than 'simply' quantifying the financial results. It deepens and enriches our insight into the most important value drivers of the business. What are the most sensitive points and what effects do these have on implementation of a strategy, for example? In what way does the financial performance of the same option vary in different scenarios and what are the major risks?

Standard models?

Elaborating a financial model is always time consuming and sometimes also frustrating. This is certainly the case for anyone doing it for the first time. It not only demands sufficient knowledge of financial theory but also substantial practical skill in the use of the spreadsheet program. Thus the question is often asked: 'Why isn't there a standard model, where all we have to do is to type in the figures?' The answer is simple: standard models only work in standard situations. A good financial model is so specific to the case contained in the central question that a standard model will not suffice.

But however specific one has to be, it helps to have experience of building a financial model. The avid learner is best advised first to study the financial models from other strategy projects. It also helps if an experienced person takes a look in order to pass on their know-how and practical tips. Finally, it is also a sensible idea not to just launch yourself into modelling but to think hard about it first and consider the aims, the limiting values and the specifications of the model.

The goal of this period is to make a good financial model, one that serves as a tool for comparing the options with each other within the different scenarios and for understanding and evaluating each option in detail. Such a financial model is nearly always made to measure, as it is specific to the case contained in the central question. Thus you need to create a new financial model in virtually every strategy project.

Step 1   Determine the aims and output of the model

What exactly do we want to test with the model? This is the most important question for defining the specifications of the financial model. The model's output must, after all, be in line with the desired financial aims. The answer is not always trivial. One of the aims is nearly always to compare the net present value (NPV) of the options within the various scenarios. However, there are often other aims. What are total capital needs for all necessary investments before the business generates a positive cash flow? What does this mean for the asset liability relations and financing opportunities?

In addition the model must offer a detailed insight into the timing of the NPV and *its* composition. Does a major part of the value lie far off in the future or will an important part be achieved in the short term? Where does the cash flow come from? Which markets, channels, client segments, product types and/or service levels are important? The options also give hints as to the most important insights that the model should offer. Are the most important improvements a result of prices, commercial strength, operational efficiency or the reduction of overheads?

The aims are then translated into the model output, for which the three most important financial overviews form the basis: the calculation of results, the balance sheet and an overview of cash flows (with a calculation of the NPV). The aims determine how these data are to be entered in detail. This requires basic knowledge and sufficient understanding of financial theory in order to be able to make the necessary choices. In the case of the calculation of results, for example, filling in the main points may sometimes be enough, whereas in other cases it is necessary to make a detailed division into channels and products. The same sort of thing is true for the balance sheet. If only the development of capital employed is important, you can sometimes make do with the net assets, without having to look at the financing aspect. If, however, existing bank loans might be at risk, you probably need for your output a detailed model of a complete balance sheet in accordance with current accounting standards.

A usable financial model is a *nominal* model, that is, including inflation. Don't be tempted to leave inflation out of the financial model (costs and earnings both exclude inflation, so it doesn't matter). This model, known as a *real* model, nearly always leads to errors and confusion.

Step 2   Select input variables and suppositions

It is important with every model to choose the input variables carefully. It is of course impossible to calculate all possible alternatives and effects in model form. Which situations *should* the model be able to deal with? The differences between the options and the scenarios determine in effect which input variables are necessary. If the price of raw materials is an important parameter in the scenario the model must be able to evaluate the effects of variation in these prices. If one of the options is to close a factory it must be possible to use the model to work out the effects of this step. Comparing the options and the scenarios with one another is thus *the* way of obtaining a clear picture of the minimum number of input variables necessary for the model.

However, there are often other inputs for the model as well. All suppositions that are important in determining the NPV constitute an input, even if they have not been defined separately in the options or in the scenarios. Inflation, exchange rates and the required return on investment are common examples. There are a number of advantages in treating these 'value drivers' as input variables. First, it is a good idea to make these kinds of suppositions explicit, precisely because they strongly affect the model results and thus the interpretation of those results. Second, it is possible to start programming the financial model before the values for these suppositions have been put in. Finally, the model remains usable if these suppositions change later on.

Once all the input variables are known, the possible values are put in. The options and scenarios also give the lead here. It is relatively easy to determine the values of the input variables if the options and scenarios have been defined in enough detail. Making meaningful choices for factors such as inflation, exchange rates and especially the required return on investment is a discipline in itself and falls outside the scope of this book.

Step 3 Structure the model

Now that the output and the input have been defined, the model can be structured. What are the various parts of the model and how do they relate to one another? If the closure of a factory is an option it is useful to model separately the operational costs of the factory (and the costs of closure). The operational costs of other factories where such questions do not arise could perhaps be modelled as one whole. In doing this you must still take into account the possibility of letting the variable costs rise, in case the production volume from the factory selected for closure is transferred to one of the other factories.

Establish an unambiguous and transparent connection between the input variables and the output that has been defined. A transparent structure helps to keep the workings of the model clear and helps you to avoid mistakes. If you avoid any ambiguity the structure of the model will guarantee, for example, that the input variables cannot in any way depend on the output. This last point looks obvious but this is one of the key challenges (and risks) in constructing a financial model. An example will make this clear.

For many products and services the development of the market price (certainly in the short term) does not depend, for example, on the variable (i.e. the avoidable) production costs. Thus there does not seem to be any necessity for a relationship between these two parameters in the structure of the model. But suppose that there is pressure on prices and that we expect the variable costs to rise? Over time the price could drop below the level of the avoidable production costs, which is unlikely in a business economic sense. In the long term, or with other starting values, there is then a direct relationship between these two parameters. It is in any case not always advisable to include this in the model structure. Sometimes things become so complex that it is more pragmatic to limit variation in the input variables.

One important choice to make is how many years ahead the financial model should look. This is determined to a great extent by the answer to the question of how far into the future we can still make meaningful forecasts.

Pitfall: failing to take account of price erosion

In many sectors continuing improvements in productivity, together with strong competition, ensure a continuous decline in price levels in real terms (adjusted for inflation). However, this price erosion is often not shown in financial models. Today's prices are used for future prices, possibly more for the sake of convenience than out of conviction. After all, it's only a matter of a few percentage points per year.

However, leaving out a few percentage points of price erosion per year is enough to send profitability through the roof. A company with a net margin on turnover of 8%, and which expects an annual rise in productivity of 3%, will see their company results at least doubling in five years in the model if price erosion is not included.

Just how much does this price erosion amount to? If we are in no way cleverer than the competition and if we fail to gain any structural advantage over our competitor, the answer to this question is that price erosion is probably very close to 3% per year. In all probability it will not be zero.

This can vary according to the industrial sector or the individual situation but in practice it is rare that you can model in any detail more than five years ahead. Of course a business option still has value at the end of the period covered by the model. You must be extremely careful in determining what is known as the 'end value'. People often use a formula based on an infinite series of annual cash flows. Take good note of the fact that this does not imply any real growth. After all, it is never the case that a company's free cash flow grows infinitely each year.

Step 4   Programme the model and check how it works

Now it is time to programme the model using a spreadsheet programme. This requires above all sufficient familiarity with the programme, and there are also a number of useful 'rules of behaviour'. Make sure that you have a clear structure and layout, so that fellow team members can read it too. Implement the model structure 'physically' in the spreadsheet application: use separate tab sheets for the input variables, intermediate results and for each of the outputs (calculation of profit and loss, balance sheet and cash flow overview).

A common mistake of beginners is to save the various options and scenarios in different file versions of the financial model. This never works in practice, as it is always necessary to make changes to the model. Always work with one file for the financial model and make sure that the various options and scenarios can easily be swapped around within that file. Do make sure that the names of the options and scenarios that are being modelled at a particular moment are listed on all output sheets so that it is immediately clear how the results should be interpreted.

It is easy to make a mistake in programming the model. Such an error can have major consequences and it can sometimes take days before it is discovered and corrected. For this reason work very conscientiously and do not let yourself be distracted. Record what you do and always finish one step completely before starting on something else. Be circumspect about replacing value-generating formulae with fixed numbers (even if it is just for a quick check). If your model is also used by other people, make sure that they cannot cause any damage by making as many cells as possible in the spreadsheet unalterable. If possible have another team member check whether all the formulae have been copied consistently.

Once the model has been programmed, it must be tested. How does the output change in response to variations in the input? Can you see how these changes are derived and are they explicable? Is it clear how the model incorporates variations in the inputs? For this, look also in detail at the interim results. Allow sufficient time for testing the model as this often reveals a few more small errors. Try also to 'crash test' the model. What happens when you use unrealistically large or small input values? Can you still explain the outcomes or has the model reached its limits? How does the model then react?

Step 5   Interpret the model results (make final changes if necessary)

The model is now ready for use. Following the more 'technical' tests in the previous step, it is now the turn of the 'business economic' test. Combine the various options and scenarios and try to interpret and explain the results. This often leads to new, unexpected insights and a better understanding of the business economics. As an example, the gross margin is shown to decline in spite of the fact that the price of the most important product is rising. The explanation could be that there is much more growth available from low margin products, which greatly changes the product mix.

This step sometimes leads to a few last-minute changes. Now that we understand much better how everything affects everything else, certain suppositions appear less probable or we can see that the structure as it has been programmed is still not as good as it could be. Once the financial model is finally completely finished, the strategic choices can be underpinned financially. All the hard work done previously on the various analyses now makes the work a piece of cake. Thanks to the well-presented layout, copies of the output sheets can be sent directly to the steering committee if necessary.

15

Days 58 to 60 – We choose the strategic direction

What is the goal for these days?

During these days the spotlight is on the senior managers, who will select a strategic direction for the company based on the work done by the team. The team has no control over how they do this, as it will be determined by the company's procedures and traditions governing such matters.

There are a number of ways in which the team can offer to help with the selection process. The most obvious is to have a discussion session in which the qualitative and quantitative aspects of the various business options can be addressed. The team can then explain the options in more detail. The following questions might come up in the discussion:

- Why should this option allow us to 'win the game'? In what way are we different from the competition?

- What is the nature and size of the company in this option? What skills need to be developed and how do we do that? What style and mentality are needed in our staff? Does this suit us and is it achievable?

- What kind of reactions can we expect from our shareholders, from employees and from trades unions?

- How do we deal with the uncertainties? What risks are we willing to take and what can we do to limit the risks?

The corporate centre: its role and value creation

Most of the analyses and examples in this book relate to business unit strategy. For this reason we would like to look in more detail within this context at *corporate* strategy and the role of the *corporate centre.*

Corporate centres are often associated with conglomerates and it is partly for this reason they have come under fire in recent years. Companies are always being advised to concentrate on their core activities, to reverse the diversification of the 1970s and to split the business into separate companies, each focused on a single sector. The corporate centre within such a conglomerate is said not to offset its own costs through value creation within the business units. It is even accused of destroying value by discouraging or frustrating entrepreneurial drive in the business units. Diversified companies are therefore urged to make their various activities independent and to disband their corporate centre.

However, this sort of advice too easily misses the necessity – or in many cases the inevitability – of a corporate centre, even in companies that are active only in one sector or in one product group. It can be necessary due to size (*span of control*), because the company serves several client segments (often with differing business models) or because the company is active in several different countries (often with differing market characteristics and competitive positions). These factors cause the company to divide automatically into a number of smaller companies. These companies' activities need to be co-ordinated and investment resources need to be divided up among them. Thus, the question should not be *whether* a corporate centre is necessary, but rather what role the corporate centre should play in order to add value to the various businesses.

Richard Koch[1] identifies five legitimate strategies, as he calls them, with which the corporate centre can add value.[2] Let us run through them briefly.

[1] Koch, R. (1995). *The Financial Times Guide to Strategy: How to Create and Deliver a Useful Strategy.* Englewood Cliffs, NJ: Prentice Hall.
[2] Koch in fact identifies six strategies, but the first on his list, the corporate emergency strategy, is not covered here as it is not really a separate strategy, but rather an ad hoc intervention by the corporate centre in the business units to address sudden, pressing problems that the business units cannot solve by themselves.

The Olympian strategy

In this strategy the corporate centre is of minimal size, consisting of a CEO who devotes most of his or her time to decentralised tasks (such as the part-time management of one of the business units) and a minimal financial staff that consolidates and reports on the business units' results in order to fulfil legal requirements. Although the role of the corporate centre in such a set-up is very limited, it can add substantial value. With a good understanding of the underlying activities and insight into the quality of the managers, it can intervene in a business unit if necessary to replace a failing management. This is the origin of the name: the Greek gods on Mount Olympus paid very little attention to the human world, but when they did intervene they were rigorous and merciless.

The acquisition-driven strategy

In the acquisition-driven strategy the corporate centre adds value through successful acquisitions. This is not as simple as it sounds, as research shows again and again that most acquisitions create little or no value for the purchaser: synergies are overestimated and risks ignored; this leads to excessively high prices that only benefit the shareholders of the acquired company. Successful private equity companies do, however, provide daily proof that value can be created through acquisitions. They succeed because they are good at selecting and judging the most suitable takeover candidates, and because they follow a very structured and standardised post-acquisition path, which allows them quickly to realise the potential for financial improvement offered by the acquisition. A corporate centre with the acquisition skills of a good venture capitalist can thus create considerable value.

The market expansion strategy

In the market expansion strategy the corporate centre focuses on one goal: to achieve a dominant position in each of the company's areas of activity. The corporate centre ensures that the company is only active in fields where it is either already the market leader or where it can use its position in related markets to become the leader. The company does not invest in activities where this is not possible. The market expansion strategy is thus a rather extreme version of the classic portfolio strategy. Properly executed, this strategy delivers carefully targeted but significant expansion in those parts of the market where the company can achieve above-average results.

The competence and culture building strategy

As the name suggests, the success of a competence-based strategy depends on a company possessing a distinguishing capability that can lift the operations within its various activities to a higher level. This capability could be a special business culture, a unique skill or a technological advantage. The role of the corporate centre is to spread this unique capability around the business units, to guard and strengthen this capability single-mindedly in all parts of the organisation. The competence-based strategy is unfortunately not for every company but many of the world's best-known and consistently high performing organisations have attained their leading positions in just this way.

The performance control strategy

In this strategy the corporate centre sets itself up as a financial watchdog, but one with above-average insight into the potential for financial improvement. By simplifying operations, disseminating commercial best practices and imposing healthy financial discipline, the corporate centre is able to boost the performances of the underlying business units. Some companies manage to create significant value by using this strategy in conjunction with the acquisition-driven strategy, with the corporate centre immediately incorporating new acquisitions into its performance-enhancing drive.

There are extraordinarily successful examples for each of the strategies described above. Sadly there are also corporate centres that have not succeeded in making the chosen strategy work for their company. This is sometimes because the corporate centre makes the wrong choice, one that is not appropriate to the company. More often, failure is due to the lack of a clear choice or because the chosen strategy is only implemented in a half-hearted way.

16

Days 61 to 65 – We write the strategic plan

What is the goal for these days?

A choice has been made but part of the organisation does not yet know it. And if we do not write it down, in a few months' time nobody will know it. That is why we write a strategic plan.

Every self-respecting organisation has a strategic plan. It is not usually a gripping read, but why shouldn't it be a real page-turner? After all, many members of staff find it quite a pleasant pastime to philosophise over where the company should be heading. Then a plan arrives – a plan that offers direction, with plenty of supporting evidence, and yet it is not exciting to read. Strange, isn't it?

We would dare to suggest that most strategic plans do not do what they are supposed to do. They are not clear and concise and do not offer a distinctive path to follow. What is wrong with these plans? We can offer three theories:

- Whoever said that strategic plans had to be such massive doorstops? Where did the idea come from that a strategic plan has to contain an exhaustive description of the market, our production sites and our shops? Why so much information when a large part of it doesn't help to support the arguments at all? What do we want with all those graphs and tables? What do we learn from those endless SWOT analyses?

- Why are the most important points missing from most plans? Points such as: 'How do we distinguish ourselves from the competition?' or: 'How do we win the game?' The plan just suggests a pinch more of this and a touch more of that, but what is our real strength? The plan also often lacks a financial perspective. Are we also supposed to earn something by using this strategy? Sometimes one simply has to guess at the answer.

- The more exhaustively the background is described, the shorter the plan becomes when it attempts to describe the strategic direction to take. Some plans offer no more than a mission statement. We want to be a fantastic organ-isation for our customers, our employees and our share-holders. We want to operate in a socially responsible way. We are going to make everyone's life better and we will be a customer-friendly organisation, and so on. The big question still remains: how? Be specific.

We should like here to argue in favour of a concise and conclusion-orientated strategic plan. Such a plan is made up of three sections. Each section can be divided into chapters according to taste.

Background

This section explains why we want to do something, why there are choices to be made and how urgent it is. It indicates briefly what our position is. What has improved or worsened recently? What trends do we see in the market, which we need to respond to? What (latent) demand can we take advantage of? In short, why is there a new strategy?

Strategy

Come straight to the point. Explain what direction we are choosing, what we are going to do, and justify it. First, make the choices, then justify them, otherwise the reader doesn't know what to do with all the information. Only present market analyses, SWOT analyses and the like where they are essential for defending the arguments. The rest should go straight to the appendices or to the archive.

Financial forecasts

What are we going to invest in this strategy and what are we going to earn from it? What are the risks and how do we finance the strategy?

Strategy and organisational structure

Intuitively one can immediately see that a company's strategy and its organisational structure are strongly connected. A low cost airline has a much more horizontal and streamlined organisation than a full-service flagship carrier. A sales-orientated organisation divided according to customer segments will quickly find success with a strategy of cross-selling, while a product-orientated company will have more success if it promotes the key distinguishing characteristics of its products. A fast-growing retailer can be well served by having a franchise structure, which is less of a burden on the central organisation and in which the franchisees carry some of the financial risks. On the other hand, a more mature retail chain may find such a network of local franchisees is actually responsible for a lot of costs and makes it more difficult to carry out the regular format changes that are needed.

The above examples immediately prompt a kind of chicken-and-egg question: Which came first, the structure or the strategy? Or, on a more concrete level: Does the organisational structure determine which strategic choices are made or does the structure, or a change in the structure, emerge as a result of the chosen strategy?

This discussion was sparked in 1962 by Alfred Chandler.[1] Chandler carried out historical research into major US

[1] Chandler, A.D. (1962). *Strategy and Structure: Chapters in the History of the American Industrial Enterprise.* Cambridge, MA: MIT Press.

companies and concluded that they adapted their organisational structure to changes in market demand. General Motors, for example, was forced to change from a functional, centralised organisation to a looser structure with separate divisions in response to demand from the market for a greater variety of products.

This theory has been regularly attacked ever since, usually with the argument that in practice organisations do not operate rationally and are thus not capable of making rational choices. Our own experience has taught us that companies do indeed have difficulties in making strategic choices and implementing the resulting structural changes. In many cases, however, a strategic change that is not, or not fully, implemented represents only a stay of execution for the company as it will have to take similar measures later on, often under more difficult financial conditions. A company will ultimately only survive if it can operate in the market with a viable strategy and can adapt its structures to that strategy.

A typical approach to a strategy project confirms the adage that *structure follows strategy*. First, the key strategic choices are investigated and evaluated. Only once a decision has been made does the company work out a suitable organisational structure. However, we must temper this primacy of the strategy with a few comments:

- A viable strategy and an organisational structure appropriate to it are no guarantee of success. The extent to which a company is able to carry out the strategy effectively and, in the long term, adapt it to new market conditions, depends a great deal on the quality of individual members of staff (management and other staff), but also on the characteristics of the company, both as regards its structure and its culture.

- Not every strategy is a realistic option for every organisation. Converting a discount clothing store into a luxury shop stocking the top brands would appear to be an impossible task. Not only would it be a problem for it to position itself convincingly in the market, but the necessary skills for such a proposal (composition of the product range, shopfitting, level of service, etc.) are lacking and would be difficult to acquire. It is important in a strategy project to identify as quickly as possible such so-called showstoppers for a strategy under investigation.

Structural changes take up time and money. You can develop a new strategy in three months but reorganisations often take more than a year, require a lot of attention from management and involve considerable costs (recruitment and layoffs of staff, moving to a new location, etc.). In some cases these factors can play a decisive role when a company is weighing up two alternative strategies, for instance in deciding whether it should develop particular activities itself or look for partners. In times of extreme market conditions (for example, during the e-commerce boom) the time horizon for strategic choices is so limited and so uncertain that structures can no longer be adjusted to match the strategies. Filling in the gaps in the structure then becomes an important part of the longer-term strategy, in which there is certainly more scope for flexibility.

17

Allware: make a choice and carry on

ENNY AND HER TEAM ARE NEARING THE END OF THE PROJECT. They have cracked the hardest analytical nuts and found solutions to all the pressing problems. Since the interim presentation, which went so badly, the team has managed to keep the most important decision-makers on board. In a crucial presentation to the shareholders (the family), Schmidt lets the country managers themselves present the solutions that have been found – while Jenny listens anxiously in the wings, worried that the managers will not prove to be as convinced as they have said they are. Once this exciting meeting has been concluded without any mishaps and the family has expressed their belief in the solutions the team has come up with, Jenny is enthusiastically received by her team and by Schmidt. They are nearly there. The 'only' thing they have to do now is to set out these solutions in a coherent strategy and produce an implementation plan. Surely that can't be difficult after all the challenges of the last months? But it seems that their troubles are not yet over.

Choosing what can be done

Each member of the team has developed a financial forecast for their segment. When the group controller had added all these up, it showed that Allware could indeed count once again on considerable growth in turnover and profit. In the longer term, that is. As things stand, results are set to fall further in the year ahead. The plans for the heating market of course require major investments and the shipping sector, due to falling prices, will be happy if it can maintain the same level of profit in the current financial year. Even the first key supplier contracts will only be marginally profitable under the new set-up. In fact, the company can only expect immediate improvements in results in the offshore sector.

'We need to sow before we can reap,' Jenny tells the CEO, but he is not happy about it. The family has high expectations in the wake of the country managers' presentation. Will they – and he – get the chance to reap the harvest?

'First of all, line up all the possibilities for me,' Schmidt asks. 'Surely you learned about scenario analysis at business school?'

Naturally Jenny knows how to do that. Together with her team she constructs three strategic alternatives, working by the book. These are 'Carry on cutting' (in which the company continues its cost-cutting policies of the previous years), 'Improve everything at once' (in which all plans for improvement are implemented as quickly as possible) and 'First save, then spend' (in which the company starts with the improvement plans that can produce quick results before implementing the others). These three alternatives are worked out for three possible sets of conditions – 'Stable markets', 'Watchful competitors' and 'Bad things come in threes'.

Although Schmidt finds these last three names in particular rather florid (and has them changed to the safe but boring best case, base case and worst case scenario for the presentation to the family), he is very satisfied with the outcome of the analysis. It appears that the 'Improve everything at once' alternative should create the most value but is also the riskiest of the three. In the worst case scenario Allware would actually have to get through two cash-negative years and appeal to the family for additional financing. That is not possible under the present circumstances and Schmidt chooses the safe path. The company will first take measures that will immediately produce positive results, then use those positive results to finance the other measures. The choice is thus 'First save, then spend'.

Passing the baton – and receiving new ones

There is one more important task waiting for Jenny and her team: preparing the implementation of the plan. Some of the team members will themselves be playing an important role in the implementation. Isabelle is to set up and manage the network of Allware Service Centres. Thorsten will get the sourcing of parts for offshore projects in China (and their certification in Europe) off the ground. For the others it will be time to look for new challenges.

Jenny will also be looking for something new. She has had a few extremely intensive and exciting, but also unusually instructive, months. She has also got a serious taste for strategy formulation. Luckily, as the brand-new 'Corporate Strategy Manager', she should have ample opportunity to put into practice what she has learned. She will then discover that each project offers totally different analytical and procedural challenges. She will also learn, however, that the basic approach (determine the *real* question and divide it into parts, formulate hypotheses and subject them to a well-focused analysis, make definitive choices on the basis of a thorough financial comparison) always gives good results. She discovers too that she gets better and better at making the Allware organisation follow her in this approach, until it becomes second nature.

Part IV – The implementation phase

Introduction

THE THREE MONTHS ARE OVER. THE SENIOR MANAGERS have made a well-founded choice for a strategic direction. The strategy team has worked hard and is satisfied with its results – results on paper only, for the time being. A decision has been made, but nothing has changed within the organisation yet. The implementation is yet to come (see Figure IV.1), a phase which is usually far from simple.

It is clearly difficult to change course and it takes a lot of time and effort. Although of a different nature, the challenge of carrying out a strategy is definitely not inferior to that of formulating it. We have been warned. Why then do things nevertheless so often go wrong during the implementation phase? Here are several common stumbling blocks:

The structure of the book

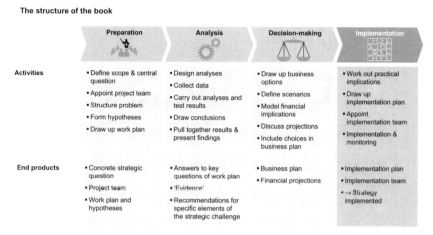

	Preparation	Analysis	Decision-making	Implementation
Activities	• Define scope & central question • Appoint project team • Structure problem • Form hypotheses • Draw up work plan	• Design analyses • Collect data • Carry out analyses and test results • Draw conclusions • Pull together results & present findings	• Draw up business options • Define scenarios • Model financial implications • Discuss projections • Include choices in business plan	• Work out practical implications • Draw up implementation plan • Appoint implementation team • Implementation & monitoring
End products	• Concrete strategic question • Project team • Work plan and hypotheses	• Answers to key questions of work plan • 'Evidence' • Recommendations for specific elements of the strategic challenge	• Business plan • Financial projections	• Implementation plan • Implementation team • → Strategy implemented

Figure IV.1   Phase 4: Implementation

- *Senior management does not fully support the plans*

  Strong management is essential for a successful implementation. Management must not radiate doubt regarding the path chosen. Any toning down by management of the strategy, the goals set or the solidity of deadlines gains force further down in the organisation.

- *Communication failure*

  Communication is an important aspect of implementation. You need to inform people both inside and outside the company about what, why and when, and, most importantly, you must communicate frequently. Failure to communicate may well be the main shortcoming of failing implementation plans.

- *The implementation team starts from scratch*

  In the three preceding phases we moved from the general to the particular. This resulted in the selection of one specific course of action. However, the rest of the organisation is less familiar with the background of the choices made. Those who were directly involved are well aware of why a specific course was chosen and what it entails exactly. An implementation team which did not experience the preceding phase will often be inclined to develop the strategy all over again and repeat the work. After all, it's fun to think about a strategic direction. Even in the fortuitous event that this were to lead to the same outcome – which is far from certain – we would lose a lot of time.

- *Resistance is not taken seriously*

There will be opposition; changes nearly always spark resistance. Positions are at stake and unfamiliarity with the newly chosen course causes uncertainty. It is best not to combat resistance with purely defensive tactics. Some criticisms may be valuable and may generate useful suggestions for converting the strategy into measures on the ground.

- *Capacity shortage*

Implementation takes up staff time. Expecting staff and middle management to be able to carry out the implementation alongside their normal work ('Managing, isn't that the usual work of managers?') is asking for trouble. If the organisation were able to handle this on the side, it would mean that we are overstaffed.

So we will address the issue of implementation separately. The implementation phase is not included in the three-month period – it may take a year or longer – but it has a decided influence on the results. For our purpose, implementation is taken to mean the implementation of the chosen strategy. This description is practical and focuses on the structure of the process. How do you set implementation in motion, how do you control such a process? We will not give any factual advice here. We will not address the challenges of cultural and behavioural changes. We will not go into detail on how to gauge the skills of current staff, or how to introduce a new role for them. And, if necessary, you will have to consult the literature on the many theories regarding alternative organisational structures. A concise description of these aspects of the process of change would fail to do the subjects justice.

For clarity's sake, we are discussing the implementation phase at the very end, after the strategy has been formulated. In practice the distinction is usually less clear. Especially in complex, dynamic surroundings, strategy determination and implementation usually occur more or less simultaneously, interactively. During the implementation phase, there may be developments which demand a strategy adjustment. The final strategy may therefore differ from the one chosen.

18

Set up an organisation to implement the strategy

What do we wish to achieve?

In the broadest sense, the implementation organisation is the team which puts the strategy into practice (to avoid misunderstandings, we don't mean the organisation itself after the implementation). This implementation organisation has little in common with our strategy team in the preceding three phases. The project team at that time consisted of three to five brains in a team room, while the implementation organisation consists of a far larger number of staff members. Sometimes hundreds of employees throughout an organisation are responsible for converting the strategy into measures on the floor of their department. They are part of the implementation organisation, but also remain involved in the line organisation. This means that they are not, as was the case with the members of the strategy team, temporarily released from the line organisation.

First of all, the relationship between the members of the implementation team and the line organisation must be determined. The individual team members must then be recruited. How will we set about this?

Step 1   Determine the relationship between line organisation and project organisation

Which organisation will actually be responsible for implementing the strategy? Will it be the existing line organisation, or will we set up a separate project organisation? Or will we opt for something in between? There are three options.

The current line organisation implements the strategy

The team members (staff members in charge of implementation) are first of all part of their existing line organisation. The line organisation itself provides progress reports, through the existing hierarchy. This has the advantage that, as far as possible, implementation forms part of normal work and that those involved have the chance to get used to the effects of the changes. A disadvantage is that it is more difficult to follow and control progress. There is ample room for 'mutiny'.

The current line organisation implements, under the leadership of a project organisation

The staff members dealing with implementation are still primarily part of their line organisation, but an active project organisation plays a coordinating role. It discusses results directly with the implementation staff and provides comprehensive progress reports to management. This gives a better view of the progress made than in the previous model. The danger, however, is that the project organisation, which has no fundamental responsibility for content, quietly turns into a purely process-orientated body which no longer has the slightest idea what it's all about. A project organisation like this sometimes develops into a paper tiger primarily based on bureaucratic procedures (generating messages in the style of: 'We have not yet received a conclusion form from the idea session').

The project organisation implements

The line organisation provides team members for the project organisation (they usually have a double role) and also plays a part in supervising the content. The team members primarily form part of the project for the duration of the implementation phase. This solution is perhaps the most productive directly speaking, but it offers little chance of contributing to and establishing a basis within the line organisation ('this wasn't our idea'). Make sure that key staff members form part of the project organisation, and guard the content by setting up steering committees and groups of experts in various fields.

Choose the form which agrees best with both the implementation assignment and the organisation. The more centralised the implementation, the smaller the chances of digression and the faster change can be achieved. At the same time, the basis of the implementation becomes less firm and there are greater risks of making errors of reasoning.

Step 2   Provide staff

First of all, embed the implementation at the top. Who in the highest ranks of the organisation will bear final responsibility for the implementation and will take on the role of head sponsor for the duration of the project? Remember that the involvement of senior management is a crucial factor for success.

Next, we need project leadership on a daily basis. Depending on how the project is embedded in the line organisation and on the scale of the project, one or more project leaders and support staff are necessary, perhaps with the addition of a project secretariat. It may be wise to involve several members of the strategy team from earlier phases in the project leadership. They are familiar with the strategy's background, know what has already been done and are able to compare the results with the original goal.

Strategy implementation requires know-how. The project manager must therefore be able to assess whether an end product is in line with the chosen strategy, must be able to recognise undesirable digressions and must be able to suggest solutions in the spirit of the strategy when the literal text proves inadequate. They must be able to point new project staff in the right direction, and must recognise when current staff members are out of their depth as to content.

The project manager must therefore be in a strong position as regards both the process and the content. Don't be fooled into believing that process and content can be segregated. Having a project manager who wishes to be involved in progress management only – 'Processes are my job, I have specialists for know-how' – will not work. Managers may display a somewhat mocking attitude towards content but the added value of true process managers in this type of process is quite limited. There comes a point where they can do little more than ask others what must be done, write it down and inquire later as to whether the job has been done, without being able to judge for themselves whether the job really *has* been done. The pure, unadulterated process manager is really only suited to less complex, 'standard' tasks such as a move to a new location or introduce a new look for the company. Last, but not least, we select a team of employees who are responsible for implementing the strategy on the floor. Determine what expertise is needed, estimate where support is necessary and free the required capacity. The ideal team member for the implementation phase is an experienced employee in the very department where they are responsible for the implementation. They are up to date regarding what is going on and able to grasp the new strategy and convert it into consequences for working methods. They have sufficient credibility within the department to propagate the new course and to convince their colleagues. And, of course, the ideal team member has a practical approach.

In actual practice, the available capacity is a major hurdle for a successful implementation. No one carries out a serious implementation 'on the side'. You have to realise that other tasks must make way for the implementation. Which tasks can be put aside (temporarily), and for which tasks can outside capacity be hired?

19

Draw up the implementation plan

What do we wish to achieve?

We must now draw up a sound implementation plan. First of all we must consider what order to do things in. We must then choose a mode of operation and lay down the responsibilities, activities and deadlines. How do we go about this?

Step 1 Determine whether the new organisation can be set up right away

A new strategy may involve a new organisation, at least in part. If that is so, it may be wise to set up the new organisation right away. The strategy will then be implemented by the new organisation instead of by the old. It is always difficult to carry out new things in an existing organisation. Whereas in determining the strategy the organisational structure came last (the organisation follows the strategy), in implementation it is the other way around.

Find out whether it is possible to set up a new organisational structure, and to appoint staff members to new functions. This will immediately take away a great deal of uncertainty for a lot of employees, and will allow them to get used to their new roles.

Consider taking any employees thought to be superfluous out of the organisation immediately. Staff who are aware that they will have to leave the organisation in the longer term are usually not very productive as far as the implementation of a new policy is concerned. Is it possible, for instance, to transfer excess employees either to a mobility pool, to await new opportunities within the company, or to a job placement agency?

Step 2   Determine the order of activities

Implementing the chosen strategy involves not only a different organisation, but also a multitude of activities, such as developing new products, working on new markets, preparing acquisitions, adapting production facilities, etc. In order to set out a timetable for these activities, we will first look for a necessary or a most logical order to follow.

Take, for instance, a case in which the management of a manufacturer of electrical carpentry tools has chosen to develop products for the 'outdoor' market (lawnmowers, leaf blowers, high pressure sprayers), in order to create an entry into the distribution channel of garden centres. They expect this to lead ultimately to an increase in demand for production capacity, which can be obtained by contracting out work to third parties. Must we now work on product concepts, distribution and production all at the same time? Probably not.

In general, there are at least three possible reasons for not tackling everything at the same time.

Run times

The process involves an inherent order, which the implementation may reflect. The distribution of 'outdoor products' only becomes relevant once the new products actually exist. Because product development is expected to take at least a year, and promotion in the new distribution channels approximately three months, the former has priority. Naturally, we studied the new distribution channels extensively in the analysis phase to find out whether there is actually a demand for our products.

Mutual dependencies

All choices are interdependent. If, for example, sales of the new products do not meet expectations, there will be no need for extra production capacity in the first few years. It is therefore sensible to postpone this conditional choice for a while. As long as we can safely count on the availability of market capacity, we do not have to start selecting and contracting suppliers yet.

Significance

All things are not equally important. Isn't the market for lawnmowers far larger than that for leaf blowers? So, let us begin with the former. Determine what measures have the greatest impact on the financial results and give these priority.

Step 3   Find a balance between centralised and decentralised management

A business is not a democracy. This we have seen clearly in the first three phases of the strategy-development process. In essence, this process was centrally organised, without broad participation by the organisation. A modestly sized team carries out analyses and makes proposals, the rest of the organisation only provides input where this is of fundamental importance, and management makes the decisions. Although this approach produces sound results quickly, we must not expect the organisation to be excessively enthusiastic about implementing it. Or even to agree with it. Or, for that matter, to know anything about it at all.

Such a purely centralised approach is no longer suitable in the implementation phase. As the implementation progresses, the process increasingly affects the work of specific departments or individual employees. For instance, take a salesperson for the electrical equipment in the previous example. This person is going to have to deal commercially with garden centres. Who is best positioned to find out how we should handle this? For example, will a standardised sales visit suffice for a garden centre, or are extensive product demonstrations necessary? Sales personnel themselves in particular will be able to answer this type of question, for example by making comparisons with the independent DIY stores, one of our existing distribution channels.

In the implementation phase we partially abandon the purely content-driven, top-down-orientated approach in favour of a more bottom-up-orientated procedural approach. This approach makes a difference between task management and stimulating input from the organisation. This does not mean that the organisation will now become a democracy, or that things will be more informal. This approach differs from the strategy-development process in three ways.

More people are involved

More details need to be worked out in a larger number of areas, while the average complexity and impact of all these details is smaller. Therefore, more choices are delegated to those who are directly involved, who have the right know-how and experience.

A plan of action focuses not only on fundamental questions and analyses, but also encompasses purely procedural elements

Who decides what and when; when and how do the parties involved reach agreement; how are external experts included in the process?

A longer trajectory

A strategy whose main points took three months to formulate can rarely be implemented in three months. Count on a year or longer.

Already at this stage you should distinguish between those components of the implementation that would fit in a centralised approach, and those for which a more decentralised, process-orientated approach would be preferable. This distinction is based on three characteristics of the measure we wish to implement.

Degree of uncertainty

If we already know that we will have to pay all the more difficult accounts an average of three visits in order to penetrate the new distribution channels, a process-orientated approach is possibly not the answer. We know what has to be done in practice, so let's just do it! If, however, we haven't the slightest idea yet about the correct marketing and sales approach, a more process-orientated approach would seem advisable.

We will involve the various marketing and sales employees in the process, we will appoint (external) experts if necessary, we will define how we are going to arrive at an end product and what that end product looks like, and set deadlines. This is more of a process and has less in the way of centrally controlled content.

Impact

The greater the dependency of success on the content of the measure, the more a top-down approach is advisable. Management may be happy to leave the layout of the new factory to others, while the design of the lawnmower, which is to pave the way to the new distribution channel, will probably be discussed in the boardroom.

Basis of support

Extensive involvement may be necessary to realise parts of the strategy for which the basis of support is too limited. Are these salespeople really so eager to start working on the garden centres? But be careful: involving workers in a process just in order to 'trap' them doesn't work. Is anyone going to fail to notice that they are being fooled? Anyone who proposes broad involvement must be willing to use the input from the organisation, or the support base will never materialise.

We must organise the implementation process on the basis of such considerations. In which fields are we dealing with actual implementation, is central control of a number of clearly defined activities the best method, and in which areas should the organisation seek to fill in the strategy with the aid of broader-based involvement?

Be careful: although broad involvement in a process may be appropriate for providing missing know-how and creating a solid basis for support, it also offers more opportunities for creative divergence. There is the danger with a decentralised approach that team members will re-hash everything, or drift away from the chosen basic principles.

Step 4   Translate strategic activities into implementation assignments

Last of all, a list of tasks must be drawn up, with responsibilities and deadlines. This step is the more practical version of what we did on day 10: designing analyses. Determine what is necessary to realise the strategy. To stay with the example of the carpentry tools producer: determine the tasks necessary for gaining entry to the garden centre distribution channel, such as developing your presentation, adapting the discount and bonus structure to the traditions of that distribution channel, contracting a logistics operator suitable for these outlets, training sales personnel, drawing up a commercial address list, etc. Also, do not forget to pay attention to 'indirect', non-technical tasks such as going through legal and licensing procedures, informing all parties directly involved, training and recruiting staff.

For each activity you must specify an end product. For example, for the discount and bonus structure we will not settle for a description of what is different in the new distribution channel. The end product aimed for is a concrete, detailed proposition. Every useful activity has an end product of some sort. If not, the task is superfluous, because apparently it has nothing to offer.

Assignments without a deadline are not 'real' assignments. Make a realistic estimate of the time needed for every activity depending on, on the one hand, the means available in the organisation (how quickly *can* it be done?) and, on the other, pressure from the environment (how quickly *must* it be done?). In this phase, do not set too much store by the so-called 'pressure-cooker approach'; an artificially short run time on paper usually does not lead to accelerated operations in practice, but rather to a loss of credibility of deadlines in general.

Finally, determine who is responsible for which assignment. Responsibility must always lie with an individual, and not a department.

20

Direct progress

What do we wish to achieve?

From the very start of the strategy path we have essentially followed an intellectual process on paper. First, we decided how we were going to develop a strategy, then we formulated a strategy, and subsequently we decided how we are going to implement this strategy. There is only one thing left to do now: actually implement the strategy. From paper to reality is always a difficult step.

This step, euphemistically ranked as the third item in the fourth phase – implementation – is the toughest and without question most time-consuming of the whole process. And it is the one about which we have the least to say. We have a well-founded strategy and implementation plan, and now the time has come to carry them out. All that remains for us to do is to make three recommendations on how to direct the implementation. These are listed below. How will we set about it?

Step 1 Use a practical planning instrument

We did not place the use of planning instruments high up in the list of priorities in the analysis phase. In the implementation phase, however, they are essential. So many different assignments are no longer manageable without the aid of such instruments. The market offers a variety of standard packages. Often, however, a home-grown planning instrument based on spreadsheet or database applications will do just as well.

A planning instrument (see Figures 20.1 and 20.2) must in any case do the following things:

• Give a description of the assignment. What needs to be done? What demands will be made?

• Give a description of the expected end product and be as specific as possible.

• Name the latest possible starting date for the task to be finished before the deadline expires.

• Name the latest possible finishing date, the deadline.

Deliverables and tasks	due date	% done	% should be	responsable
1. Finalised Business plan Spain	1/3/004	97%	100%	John H.
2. Approval by Spanish authorities	11/3/2004	80%	80%	
3. Finalise selection of cities to start	15/3/2...	80%		
4. Operational shops network				
Open new shop in Barcelona		90%	90%	
Identify suited location		45%	60%	
Negotiate real estate contract		0%	0%	
Recruit new Shop manager and pe		0%	0%	
Arrange all facilities (phone, elect		0%	0%	
Identify physical changes to the		0%	0%	
Plan and execute physical ch		0%	0%	
Install furniture, displays, de 11/8/2004		50%	55%	Sara L.
Official opening of shop		100%	100%	
Open new shop in Malaga		100%	100%	
Indetify suited location		100%	100%	
Negotiate real estate co		100%	100%	
Recruit new Shop mana		80%	80%	
Arrange all facilities (fhp...)		100%	100%	
Identify physical change		100%	100%	
Plan and execute physic		100%	100%	
Install furniture, displays		45%	60%	
Deliver stock and place		0%	0%	
Official opening of shop		0%	0%	
Open new shop in Madrid				
Negotiate real estate contract		55%	55%	Sara L.
Arrange all facilities (phone, elec /8/2004		100%	100%	
Identify physical changes to the st		100%	100%	
Plan and execute physical changes		100%	100%	
Install furniture, displays, desks and eq		100%	100%	
Deliver stock and place in displays		100%	100%	
Official opening of shop		80%	80%	
5. Operational logistics network	14/7/...			
6. Operational headquarters	1/6/2004			
7. Operational F&A department	17/6/2004	75%	90%	Marc. S
8. Operational HR department	1/6/2004	90%	95%	Cathy F.
9. Operational Commercial department	14/7/2004	80%	80%	John H.

Figure 20.1 Planning tool allows implementation team to assess progress and spot issues

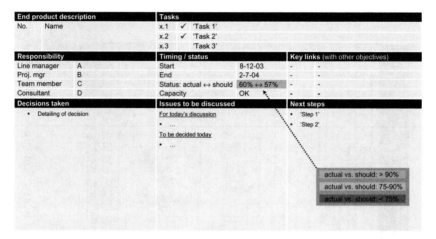

Figure 20.2 Progress and questions still outstanding should be tracked in a focused manner for each project phase

- Appoint the people responsible. Who will carry out the assignment? Who can be consulted? Who is responsible for quality control?

- Give a description of the status per assignment (percentage finished versus planned percentage finished) at the time of reporting.

- Realise that it is necessary to submit the results to a steering committee or expert group. Does the steering committee have to approve the result, or just be aware of it? Or is there another committee to which the results must be submitted?

- Pay attention to links with other tasks. Are there connections in terms of process (timing) or content (synchronisation)?

Step 2   Monitor progress and motivate the team by means of regular progress reports

A successful implementation demands strict control. Submit progress reports regularly, for example weekly or every two weeks. Under the direction of the daily project leadership, the people responsible for the various components report their decisions regarding content (which either do or do not have to be approved by the steering committee), the questions regarding content which have arisen as well as the progress made in relation to the deadlines set. The tone and style of these sessions have a strong impact on the process.

Show the involvement of senior management

Someone from senior management should preferably always be present for the regular progress reports. Keep emphasising the value of the new strategy.

Be strict regarding deadlines

As soon as deadlines start shifting, everything comes adrift. As a rule, don't accept overruns. If an overrun threatens, free more capacity or look for ways of simplifying the assignment.

Remain critical as regards process and substance

Take care that progress meetings are not just about status versus planning, but that the nature of the solutions chosen is also discussed. These sessions are definitely also to be used for checking the outcomes that have been reached. Does the proposed marketing campaign dovetail with the new proposition? How can the campaign be reconciled with the planned cutback in marketing staff? Why are the promotion expenses per outlet using the new distribution channel so much lower than in other channels – is that correct? The search for the best solution within the framework of the strategy chosen must be second nature within the project organisation and, eventually, also outside that organisation.

Be quick to solve operational problems

During the implementation phase, major and minor problems will continue to arise, problems concerning individuals, clients or undoable assignments, and rapid decision-making is essential to keep up the momentum.

Step 3   See communication as a continuous activity

Communication is *the* central theme in a successful implementation. It demands continuous attention. Develop an explicit communications strategy and include the communications department in the project. Remember that most employees are still in the dark at the end of the strategy development project.

More than just the sticking points of the strategy

Try to avoid an obsession with sore points such as the new organisational structure or redundancies. Focus communication on all points of interest concerning the new strategy:

- Specify the cause and urgency of the change. What changes in the outside world are forcing us to change our course? What is the competition up to? What are the consequences if we do nothing? How much time do we have?

- Explain the new course with regard to our clients. What do we want to do differently for our clients? How does our proposition change? What external changes are we aiming for?

- Point out the consequences for the organisation. Will our internal operations have to change, will we have to organise things differently or undertake different things to realise those external changes?

- Describe the changed expectations concerning individual employees. What changes must employees effect in terms of behaviour or style? How will their job or their particular component of the organisation change?

The more the better

'Surely we communicated that clearly?' is often heard when employees prove to be not up to speed. Clearly? Maybe; but the question is: how often? For complex matters like a new strategy you must expect to have to deliver the same message many times. Some employees need to hear something no fewer than five times before the necessity of a change in strategy really sinks in. And then another five messages in order to be really convinced. And then another five to make clear how it will be done and to fire their enthusiasm. Try to vary the way of communicating (positioning, style, communication channel), but don't hesitate to repeat the content of the messages nearly verbatim. Repetition is necessary.

Success must be celebrated

Successes are also an excellent excuse for communication. Celebrate successes such as reaching a milestone or the successful introduction of a product or a system. Fly the flag so that everyone can see that the strategy works or that the implementation is progressing well. Let role models, such as successful salespeople in the new segment, have their say.

Both internal and external

Communication is aimed both at the organisation and at third parties. Take the unions seriously, and so improve chances for constructive cooperation. Also, make sure that there is a plan for communication with clients. Show that the strategy is meant to improve services. Do not deny the possibility of teething problems.

Provide communication from above to below on a regular basis. First, inform middle management, so that they can inform the rest of the organisation. Ensure that the messages in the various parts of the organisation are consistent. Be careful, because if middle management is not convinced, the employee on the floor usually won't be a believer either.

Use a variety of media. Do not just use in-house media such as the company newsletter. Send e-mails on the status of the implementation, organise lunch meetings with senior management, ensure that the implementation becomes a regular item on the agenda of staff meetings, etc. Do not let only management have a say in the company newsletter – in the ubiquitous interview, with pictures of a gesticulating manager at his desk – but also let employees give their views. What do all these changes mean for them, what do their customers say, what is their opinion of the new products?

Persuasion

Who are they, the hard-to-convince employees who will be the main target of your efforts of persuasion?

The yes-men

They say yes, but behave as if they mean no. When the deadline arrives they always say: no time, it didn't work, I didn't get the information, the task wasn't quite clear. Be strict with the yes-man. An easy-going attitude will not work.

The constant questioners

They are willing and they are interested in the new course and the ideas on which it is based. They do not avoid debate, but are never quite convinced. A new 'why' question is always just around the corner. There is always a new reason to 'just go over that again'. Make it clear at a certain point that the 'why' phase is over and that the 'do' phase has begun. Do not let yourself be endlessly drawn into debate.

The malcontents

They do not agree, but it never becomes clear exactly why not. What is clear is that they raise objections to all proposals. They put whole departments to work to find new evidence as to why something is not possible or won't work. Scarcely has one objection been dealt with than a new one is launched, after which old objections are resurrected. It is a never-ending process. The formal arguments given are probably not the true ones. Find out which (personal) motives lie behind this behaviour.

The saboteurs

They do not care for the new course and are very outspoken about this. 'If you wish to turn the organisation upside down you're welcome, but don't expect me to help.' The saboteurs are very clear as to their motives. We have to increase the pressure here, albeit without letting the saboteurs repeat their firm views all too openly. Can we think of a cosmetic concession which will allow a saboteur to return painlessly to the fold?

The 'incapables'

They may well be sympathetic, but they have a hard time understanding the message. At some point, explaining no longer works. Forget the why and focus communication on what is concretely expected from the 'incapable' employee.

Afterword

Good luck!

In the preceding pages we described how we, as strategy consultants, create distinctive, winning strategies for our clients. It is a step-by-step process, in which we start by formulating the correct central question. This is then broken up into manageable pieces to form a structured, hypothesis-driven 'issues tree' of subsidiary questions, each one linked to one or more, for the most part quantitative, analyses. Based on the results of the analyses, the strategy team draws conclusions, works out scenarios and business options, and – finally – makes strategic choices. Choices that form a real basis for a new future.

We apply this method with our clients on a daily basis, with great success. Our way of working differs in several crucial ways from the type of thing that you can read in the standard works on strategy formulation. You will, for instance, hardly ever have come across the word 'vision' in this book, not because we think that an inspiring vision is of no value to an organisation, but because really good strategies very rarely come into being on the basis of a previously formulated strategic vision. It is a good idea, however, to summarise the carefully formulated and well-founded strategy in a single inspiring sentence, which powerfully expresses the essence of the strategy and which can fire your colleagues with enthusiasm. The vision is the *finishing point*, though, not the *starting point*.

You will also not have encountered the well-known standard strategy frameworks in this book. This is not because such frameworks never make any sense, but because they so seldom turn out to be really useful. A strategy must be made to measure. The necessary analyses are always specific and usually unique. Our job would be a lot easier if there were a list of standard analyses, which you just had to run through in order to arrive at a usable strategy. But that would also make the job a lot less fun!

Because that is something that we also hope to have achieved. We hope not only to have shown that formulating a winning strategy is a structured process that demands discipline and – frequently – hard work, but also that hard work brings rewards. One reward comes after the project, when the company is equipped with a strategy that will really help it to progress. There are also rewards during the project, when the team keeps making surprising discoveries, undermining old beliefs and finding new solutions to well-known problems. It is a real voyage of discovery, which provides a wealth of inspiration every single day – for us in any case. We therefore wish you not only good luck but also a lot of fun along the way!

Profile of OC&C Strategy Consultants

THE METHODS AND EXAMPLES IN THIS 'STRATEGIC cookbook' were not concocted while sitting behind a desk. They emerged from the advisory experience of OC&C Strategy Consultants, where they are used on a daily basis to help clients find solutions to challenging, strategic problems. Here is a brief profile of the company.

Using an international network . . .

OC&C Strategy Consultants is an international strategic advice company, working from offices in Brussels, Dubai, Düsseldorf, Hamburg, Hong Kong, London, Mumbai, New York, Paris, Rotterdam, San Francisco and Shanghai.

. . . to create value . . .

OC&C Strategy Consultants aims to help clients achieve noticeable and lasting improvements in their performance. To this end they seek new sources of growth and increased margins, then develop strategies to realise such growth and higher margins. These strategies are sometimes radical and often creative, but always practical and feasible. It is a unique combination of focused problem solving, feasibility and intensive involvement.

. . . for our clients . . .

OC&C's clients are large multinational corporations, private equity firms and national governments. Projects are always carried out with and for the senior management of a company: for executives who join OC&C in the search for new solutions, who do not shy away from the truth, and who are prepared to take radical steps. Such executives inspire OC&C to find solutions to the fundamental problems of their organisations.

. . . with fact-based analyses . . .

Creativity, intuition and even – up to a point – dreams are necessary in order to discover new paths. But they are not enough. For this reason OC&C's recommendations are quantified and rooted in realistic business economics. Not because facts lead automatically to solutions, or because figures tell the whole story, but because strategies that ignore facts are often wide of the mark; they are not practicable or are counterproductive.

. . . translated into clear, workable strategies

A clever answer to an important question does not in itself improve the performance of a company. A polished presentation is not the same as implementation; a clever report does not automatically lead to a change of course. OC&C is committed to translating the agreed strategic choices into concrete measures and visible improvements. This requires 'getting under the skin' of the client to share their concerns and successes. OC&C's consultants continue to support their clients in implementing the strategies that they have developed, and this over a period of years, in the context of a close relationship between the client and OC&C.

Index

80/20 rule 99–100
acceptability, outcomes 93, 101, 109
acquisition-driven strategy 212–13
acquisitions *see* takeovers
age, customers 142–3
agendas
  kick-off session 37
  presentations 169
airline industry 16–17, 105–8
Allware case study
  analysis phase 171–80
  decision-making phase 221–3
  implementation plan 223–4
  introduction xxv–xxviii
  preparation phase 79–87
analyses
  business economics 65–72
  business segmentation 96–9
  customer behaviour 59–62
  market understanding 62–5
  operational performance 72–5
  outcomes testing 136–40
  priorities 99–101
  questions 57–75
  types 101–12
  work plan 57–78
analysis phase xxiii, 89–180
  Allware case study 171–80
  conclusions 140–5, 149–69
  data collection 117–33
  methods 95–115
  presentations 149–69

  purpose 92
  testing 135–40
  work plan 145–7
anecdotes 53
annual reports 13, 74, 128
approximation 131–3
averages 60–1, 99
avoidable costs 66, 68–71

background section, strategic plan 217
balance sheets 200–1
bar graphs 164–5
behaviour
  competitors 20–1
  customers 59–62
benchmarking 104–8
blame avoidance 54
bottom-up approach 110–11, 241
brainstorming 24–5, 42–5
bureaucracy 77–8
business options
  Allware case study 222–3
  financial models 202–3
  formulating 185–92
  implementation 230
  scenarios 193–8
business unit strategy xiii–xiv
businesses
  data collection 127–8
  economics 65–72
  revolutions 14–19
'buy-in' 151, 158

calculations
data estimation 131–3
financial models 201–2
validity 138
capacity
implementation phase 229, 236
price link 70–1
capital-intensive sectors 68–71
case study
analysis phase 171–80
decision-making phase 221–3
implementation phase 223–4
introduction xxv–xxviii
preparation phase 79–87
cash flows 200–1
celebrations 254
central question
formulation 7–25, 81–2
issue trees 39–50
centralisation 240–4
Chandler, Alfred 218–19
characteristics
effective teams 34
end products 114
planning instruments 248–50
team members 30, 235
choices
decision-making phase 183–4
problem-solving approach xviii
strategy decisions xv
see also business options
clients see customers
column graphs 164–6
commitment, management 24–5, 87
communication
implementation phase 228, 252–5
steering committee 150–2
teams 127, 144
comparisons
analysis 102–4
graphical form 164–5
slide presentations 163
competence-based strategy 213–14
competition
business impact 19–21
customer alternatives 61–2
data collection 127–8, 130–1
financial performance 13, 15
operational performance 74–5
reactions 187–8
scenarios 195
competitive strategy see business unit
strategy
completeness
business segmentation 97
issue trees 45, 49–50
concepts xiii–xvi
conclusion-orientated story 157–8

conclusion-orientated strategic plan 217
conclusions
importance 140–1, 145
presentation 149–69, 179–80
slides 160
so what question 141–4
confidentiality 121, 122
consistency
business options 186, 188–9
implementation messages 255
scenarios 197–8
consumer research 128
content, strategic plan 217
corporate strategy xiii–xiv, 210–14
correlations 163
costs
analyses 105–8
bases 66
business economics 65–75
business options 189–91
customer behaviour 61–2
data collection 120–2
mergers and takeovers 139–40
scenarios 195–6
culture building strategy 213–14
customers
age 142–3
behaviour 59–62
communication 254
information source 21, 120
research 174–7
service 18, 176

data collection 117–33
anomalies 135–6
clients 21, 120
competitors 127–8, 130–1
documentation 144
employees 128
estimation 131–3
financial 120–2
formats 120–2
interviews 122–7
mystery shopping 130–1
self-help 128–31
sources 119
databases 109, 120, 248
deadlines
data collection 122
implementation phase 245, 248, 251
maintaining 147, 251
necessity xx–xxii
work plan 76–8
decentralisation 240–4
decision-making phase xxiii, 181–224
Allware case study 221–3
option formulation 185–92
results modelling 199–208

scenarios 193–8
  strategic plan 215–17
deductive reasoning 40
delegation 147
demographic change 196
dependencies 239–40, 250
deregulation 19
design
  analyses 59–75
  slides 160–8
detail
  analyses 147
  business options 189–90
  data collection 118
  relevance 140–1
  strategic plan 216
direction, strategic plans 186,
  217
discounts 18
distinctiveness
  capabilities 213–14
  scenarios 197
distribution xvi, 17–18
documentation
  analyses 136, 144–5
  strategic plan 215–17
  see also reports
drivers
  analyses 102–3
  costs 66–7
  financial models 203
  market development 64–5
Du Pont tree 12

earnings trees 12–16, 20
economic development 195
economies of scale 67, 72–3,
  139–40
elevator pitch 141
employees
  implementation involvement 240–1,
    243–4
  information source 128
  persuasion 255 7
end products xxiii
  analyses 144–5
  formats 112, 114–15
  preparation phase 5
  tasks 33–5, 244–5
  types 145
  work plans 58
end values 206
estimation 131–3
evidence 93
exchange rates 136, 137–8, 203

factor costs 195–6
facts and figures xix, 93

feasibility
  business options 188–9
  questions 50
  scenarios 197–8
feedback 35, 122
ferry service 47–8
financial assessment
  business options 189–91
  scenarios 198
financial management 214
financial models 67, 105–8,
  199–208
financial performance analysis 11–16, 81–2,
  173–4
findings, presentation 151–60
five forces model 19
focus
  project definition 83–4
  removing irrelevancies 11
  segment analysis 100–1
  strategic plan 216
  strategy communication 253
  subsidiary questions 42–3
forecasting
  Allware case study 222–3
  comparison analysis 102–4
  driver analysis 102–3
  financial models 199–208
  market growth 63–5
  strategic plan 217
formats
  collected data 120–2
  end products 112, 114–15
  financial models 206–7
  presentations 158–60

goals
  analysis 135
  business options 185
  data collection 117–18
  financial models 199–200
  hypothesis formulation 51–2
  implementation 231–2, 237, 247–8
  issue tree 39–41
  presentations 149–50
  project organisation 27–8
  question formulation 7–8
  scenarios 193–4
  segmentation 95
  strategic choice 209–10
  strategic plan 215–17
  work plan 57–9
governing thought 155–6
graphic forms 162–8
growth
  indicators 102–3
  markets 63–5
  projections 165–6

guidelines
    financial models 206–7
    implementation 248–55
    interviews 125–6
    presentations 168–9

history
    driver influence 102–3
    financial performance 13–14, 16
    operational performance 74
hypotheses xvii–xviii
    Allware case study 85–7, 172–4,
        177–9
    formulation 51–5, 85–7
    work plans 58

implementation phase xxiii,
    225–57
    communication 252–5
    direction 247–57
    plan 223–4, 237–45, 251
    problems 227–9
    team 231–6
'incapables' 257
inductive reasoning 40, 52, 153
inflation 202, 203, 205
information sources 117–33, 144
inputs, financial models 202–3, 204
integration, service providers 18–19
intermediaries 17–18
international data 136, 137–8
Internet 17
interviews 122–7
issue trees 39–50
    Allware case study 86
    completeness 45, 49–50
    specificity 46–8, 50
    structure 45–8

key line 155–6
key suppliers 172–4
kick-off session 36–8, 84–7
Koch, Richard 211

leadership 34, 234–5
legislation 19, 195
line graphs 166–7
line organisation 232–4
linear story 153–4

malcontents 256
management
    decentralisation 240–1
    styles 34
    see also senior management
map plots 166, 168
markets
    data collection 127–8
    development 14–19, 64–5, 102–3

expansion strategy 213
    research 174–7
    understanding 62–5
MECE *see* Mutually Exclusive, Collectively
    Exhaustive
media 255
meetings
    kick-off session 36–7
    reporting sessions 36, 251–2
    steering committee 150–2
member selection, teams 29–31, 171
mergers 138–40
messages
    findings 152–3
    slides 160–2
methods
    analyses 101–12
    data collection 117–33
middlemen 17–18
milestones 254
Minto Pyramid Principle 154–7
mission xiv–xv
models
    financial 67, 105–8, 199–208
    implementation 232–4
    nominal 202
    real 202
    scenarios 198
    standard 200
    testing 137
monitoring progress 146–7, 248–52
Mutually Exclusive, Collectively Exhaustive
    (MECE) 157
mystery shopping 130–1

net present value (NPV) 201
nominal financial model 202
NPV *see* net present value

OC&C Strategy Consultants 263–5
Olympian strategy 212
operations
    effectiveness xv
    performance 72–5
    problem resolution 252
options *see* business options
organisation
    change implementation 237–8
    implementation team 231–6
    project team 27–38
    restructuring 191
outputs, financial models 201–2, 204, 207,
    208
overruns 147, 251

performance
    control strategy 214
    financial 11–16, 81–2, 173–4
    operational 72–5

persuasion
  employees 255–7
  steering committee 152
phases
  strategy development process xxii–xxiii
  see also analysis phase; decision-making
    phase; implementation phase;
    preparation phase
pie charts 164
plans
  implementation 237–45
  planning instruments 248–50
  reporting sessions 35–6
  strategic 215–17
  work 57–78, 145–6
Porter's five forces model 19
precision 101, 118, 147
preparation
  conclusions presentation 152–60
  data collection visits 129–30
  interviews 123–5
preparation phase xxiii, 1–87
  central question structuring 39–50
  first steps 7–25
  hypothesis formulation 51–5
  kick-off session 36–8
  project organisation 27–38
  question definition 7–25
  work plans 57–78
presentations
  conclusions 149–69, 179–80
  formats 158–60
  guidelines 168–9
  styles 152–60, 179–80
pressure xx, 27–8, 245
previews 151–2
prices
  business economics 68
  customer behaviour 62
  erosion 205
priorities
  analyses 99–101
  implementation plan 238–40
  strategy project 24–5
problem-solving approach xvii–xviii
problems
  implementation phase 227–9
  operational 252
  question formulation 22–3, 81–2
  segmentation 96–9
procedures, teams 31–2
process management 235
process-orientated approach 242–3
profitability 72
programming 206–7
progress
  implementation 247–52
  monitoring 146–7, 248–52
  reports 251–2

project leader 234–5
proof 93, 101
purchasing criteria 60
pyramid principle 154–7

qualitative analysis 111–14
quantitative analysis 111–14
questions
  analysis design 65–75
  formulation 7–25, 81–2
  hypothesis formulation 51–5
  implementation resistance 256
  so what 141–4
  strategic choice 209–10
  see also issue trees

ratios 138
realism 220
reasoning
  deductive 40
  inductive 40, 52, 153
  slide presentations 162
regulations 19
relevance
  analyses 146–7
  final details 140–1
  hypotheses 52–5
  question formulation 11
  slides 160–2
  subsidiary questions 45, 49–50
repetition
  communication 253–4
  implementation team 228–9
reports
  analyses 136
  annual 13, 74, 128
  implementation progress 251–2
  interviews 127
  meetings 35–6, 87, 251–2
  story writing 153–8
  strategic plan 215–17
research organisations 127
resistance, change 229, 255–7
responsibility 232–4, 245, 250
retail sector 12–16, 129–31
return on investment (ROI) 12–16,
    203
risks
  financial models 204
  implementation phase 234
  specificity 50, 52
  strategic plan 217
ROI *see* return on investment

saboteurs 256–7
sampling 109
scenarios 193–8, 202–3, 222–3
scheduling instruments 248–50
segmentation 96–9

selection
  hypotheses 55
  strategic direction 209–14
  team members 29–31, 171
senior management
  implementation phase 228, 234,
    251
  question formulation 24–5
  strategic role xvi, 209–14
  see also management
sensitivity, analyses 137
share graphs 163, 164–6
shops 129–31
skills 29–30, 234–5, 241
slides 160–8
slippage 147, 251
so what question 141–4
sources, data 117–33, 144
specialisation 17–19
specificity
  business options 190
  central question 23
  end products 114
  hypotheses 52
  issue trees 46–8, 50
  strategic plan 216
spreadsheets 109, 206–7
standard approaches 260
steering committees
  Allware case study 87
  composition 35
  conclusions presentation 149–52, 180
  implementation phase 233, 250
  meetings 36
storylines 153–8
strategic plan 215–17
structure
  business organisations 191, 210, 218–20,
    237–8
  documentation 145
  financial models 203–7
  findings presentation 153–60, 179–80
  interviews 124
  issue trees 45–8
  markets 62–3
  project organisation 28
  work plans 58
styles
  communication 254, 255
  management 34
  see also formats; structure
subsidiary questions 39–55
supply curve 68–72
supply process analysis 177–9
suppositions, financial models 203
synergy 138–40
synthesis
  business options 192
  findings 152–3

takeovers 138–40, 212–13
targeting, hypotheses 52
tasks
  allocation 75–6, 171–2, 244
  deadlines 76–8, 147, 245, 251
teams
  Allware case study 87, 171
  answer generation 54–5
  implementation phase 228–9, 231–6, 241
  information sharing 127, 144
  member selection 29–31, 171
  organisation 28, 31–6
  problem avoidance 37
  so what discussions 143
  task allocation 75–6, 244
  working space 36
technology
  competitors 75
  scenarios 196
testing
  analysis outcomes 136–40
  central question 24–5
  documentation 144
  financial models 201, 206–8
  findings 150–1
  hypotheses 52, 55
  input data 135–6
  interview conclusions 126
  issue trees 49–50
  models 137
time and motion surveys 129
time series 163–6
timescales
  financial models 205–6
  implementation plan 239, 242, 248
  maintaining 251
  required data 118
  strategy development process xix–xxii
  strategy implementation 220
top-down approach 110–11, 241, 243
trading volumes 63
trends 137

uncertainties
  business options 210
  external 194–7
  implementation plan 238, 242–3
  question formulation 42
unions 254
units, benchmarking 105

value creation xiv, 210–14
value maps 63
variables, financial models 202–3
vision xiv–xv, 260
volumes, market trading 63

'walk in the woods' 154
waterfall graphs 166–7

winning xv, 187
work plans 57–78
  analysis design 59–75
  deadlines 76–8
  revisions 145–6

task allocation 75–6
work space 36
workshops 158, 159–60

yes-men 255

Index compiled by Indexing Specialists (UK) Ltd